LETTERS TO A YOUNG TEACHER

WISDOM FOR THOSE WHO GUIDE OTHERS

PAUL O'NEILL

WITH
FRANCINNE KAYE GACILO

For Gillian

Who saw the warning signs, married me anyway, and has been quietly managing the fallout ever since.

Who reads what I meant, not just what I wrote.

Who reminds me—without (usually) eye-rolling—that wisdom isn't found in books, but in not saying "I told you so" when you're right.

Thank you for your consistent patience, your glorious laugh that turns disaster into anecdote, and your talent for making everything— especially me—more bearable.

This book may have my name on the cover, but anyone paying attention will know who kept the lights on.

Always,

Paul

For Ty and Ibet

You saved me in more ways than I can count.

You are my hearth and home – when I was still learning to feel at home within myself. You are my strength when I had none, the angels sent my way when I didn't know how to ask for help.

Thank you for lighting my way when things get dark and for loving me through all the versions I didn't yet understand.

Because of your love, I found the courage to become.

Wherever life takes me, I will carry you with me – always close, no matter the distance, no matter the years.

This is, in part, yours too.

Francinne

CONTENTS

PREFACE

FG—

Never in my wildest imagination did I think these letters would become something to be shared – read by others, printed on pages, or even be called a book. At first, I was hesitant. I thought my stories were too simple, too ordinary, too small to matter. But I was wrong. Somewhere along the way, I realised that they weren't small at all – because they were real. And real has a way of reaching people.

They began as reflections – written during slow mornings, restless nights, or while waiting for life to make sense. They were questions I couldn't ask out loud. Thoughts I couldn't name yet. They were pieces of me I could only give voice to when the inside chaos has calmed.

I wasn't looking for answers. I just needed someone to listen, someone who wouldn't hush my doubts or rush me toward a silver lining. I needed a space where I could wonder, wrestle with my own thoughts, fall apart a little until I was ready to put the pieces together again.

These conversations didn't offer neat solutions. But they offered something better – a way to stay with the questions. A way to hold the weight of things without needing to immediately understand or fix them. They made space for doubt, for reflection, for honesty. Over time, what began as simple exchanges turned into something deeper. A refuge.

Somewhere in the back-and-forth, I began to see myself more clearly. Not as someone waiting to arrive, but as someone already becoming. Looking back now, I see how these small reflections turned into something larger – a slow return to myself. With each letter, I was able to put into words what I was learning, unlearning and slowly becoming.

This book is that unfolding.

And in sharing it, my hope is simple: that somewhere in these pages, someone else might feel a little less alone. That the big questions, the distancing ache, and the liberating joys might echo something true in your own story. If even one moment here helps you see yourself with a bit more kindness, then the unfolding was worth it.

P—

When the first letter landed, I didn't leap into action. I read it twice, set it down, and made a cup of tea strong enough to resurrect the dead. There was something in the voice—unpolished;· unguarded, entirely too familiar. It didn't ask for help; it asked to be seen. And that's far more dangerous.

So, I answered. Not out of benevolence, or mentorship, or whatever saintly nonsense gets printed on retirement plaques. I answered because the questions were real, and rare is the correspondence these days that doesn't arrive with a calendar invite or a spreadsheet in tow.

What followed was not a seminar, nor a self-help safari. It was correspondence in the truest sense: *co-responsibility*. Each letter tugged a little harder on the thread. Some days we unpicked things. Other days we tied knots with more flair than function. But always, there was movement.

The strange thing is, we've never met. Different hemispheres, different decades, same inbox. Somehow, it worked.

These pages are stitched from that movement—not polished scripts, but written while the ink was still wet with doubt, exhaustion, and the occasional burst of rude clarity. No miracles here. Two people with fragile plans and full inboxes, building a scaffold of sense one paragraph at a time.

And if, while reading, you find yourself exhaling more slowly... if something warm and inconvenient unfurls in your chest like an old dog returning to its bed... well, don't be alarmed. That's what happens when someone puts words to the thing you thought you were the only one carrying.

This is a book for those who suspect that keeping it together has come at too high a cost. For the ones who are calm on the outside, and quietly screaming beneath the smile. For teachers and guides, yes— but also for anyone who has ever tried to lead while still learning how to stand.

It's not a blueprint. It's a reckoning. And if you're reading this, you're already in it. Welcome.

June 2025

ONE
THE COST OF ALWAYS BEING "OKAY"

DEAR P,

There was a time (not so long ago) when "I'm okay" rolled off my tongue so quickly. Whenever someone would ask, "How are you?", "Is everything alright?" or "Are you sure you're *really* okay?" The simple answer with an almost convincing smile, "Yes, I'm okay."

It became a reflex – a safe, polite answer I offer the world even when sometimes I was nowhere near it. I said it when I was overwhelmed. I said it when I was exhausted. I even said it when deep down I was quietly falling apart. And no one questioned it because I didn't give them reason to.

I've come to realise that "I'm okay" is always a quiet compromise we make. It's a way to protect others from our discomfort, or maybe a way to protect ourselves from the vulnerability of telling the truth. There's something easier about holding it all together. Especially when you're the one other lean on. We wear "okay" like an armour. But over time, that armour gets heavy.

The danger is, when we say "I'm okay" long enough, we start to believe that's all we're allowed to be – not too much, not too messy, not too needy. We learn to hide our sadness, our fears, our worries behind that mask. We convince ourselves that speaking up is a burden, that silence is strength, and that emotional honesty is something to reserve for later, when things settle down. But later, *unfortunately*, doesn't always come.

So, we carry on. Smiling through the ache. Functioning through the fog. And though we appear to be coping, were slowly distancing ourselves – not just from others but from our own truth. And that distance... it costs more than we think.

I think part of why we do this is survival. Somewhere along the way, we learned that showing emotion might make others uncomfortable. Or worse, it might make us look weak. So we train ourselves to manage, to minimise what we feel, and to move forward as if nothing's happening. For many of us, especially in roles where we are expected to care for others, there's an unspoken pressure to stay composed at all costs. To be the stronger one. The one who doesn't need help.

But the cost of the constant composure, or sometimes pretense, is much more than we're ready for. At first, we feel numb, a slow disconnect. We become less present, less engaged, less ourselves. We look at our social batteries as burdens. The people around us might still see us as capable, calm and composed, but deep down we begin to feel hollow.

When it becomes too much, when the weight becomes unbearable, that's when we explode. The calm, collected mask cracks. The exhaustion and tears spill out in ways we didn't anticipate. The release comes like a flood, unexpected and overwhelming. The parts of us that have been buried finally demand to be heard. We don't often realise that we're slowly losing pieces of ourselves each time we push through until it's too late. And because people are so used to hearing and seeing us "okay", they won't know when we need help.

The hardest part? We begin to forget what honesty feels like. We lose the muscle memory for connecting and opening up. Even when someone asks how we're really doing, we default to the safe answer. We might even offer a smile. Because the truth is harder to access when you've buried it under layers of "I'm okay. I'm fine. *Really.*"

And this, perhaps, is the greatest cost: when we always pretend to be "okay" we deny others the chance to truly know us, and we deny ourselves the relief of being known.

But there's another way. I learned this the hard way. I wish someone had told me earlier that being the "strong one" doesn't mean being silent or burying everything deep within. That admitting you're not okay doesn't make you less capable or any less worthy of respect. I wish I had known that reaching out wasn't a sign of weakness.

I carried too much for too long, thinking that was just what life required. And maybe that's why I'm writing this now. Because I wonder, is there a gentler way to learn this? A way to step out of the habit of pretending before it chips away at our joy, our presence, our health?

My dear friend, I know you have more wisdom to share – far wiser than mine. I hope you'd share it. Not just with me, but also to those who are still figuring out how to carry their invisible weight.

I have friends who are still caught in the rhythm of saying "I'm okay" when they are anything but. Like I was, they don't always know how to speak without fear of being judged or looking weak. Some are tired but smiling. Some are hurting but productive. All of them are doing their best – but at a cost.

So, if you have a gentler way through, please pass them on. What you've learned might just be the permission someone else has been waiting for.

With warmth and respect,

FG

Dear FG,

Let's not sugarcoat it. When people are in that place, they're in the pit. Not a cute metaphorical funk, but the proper trench-footed, breath-caught, mouth-dry, jaw-locked pit where thoughts spin like the ceiling fan in a bad motel and the only thing louder than the static in your head is the sound of silence from everyone else. Your gentle question is a big question and it's one of the biggest reasons that I do what I do.

So, welcome to the moment before the moment. The one where nothing works and everything hurts—and worst of all, you're supposed to act normal about it. You don't need rescuing. You're not a fallen sparrow.

But you do need something: a ladder. Not a moral one. A metabolic one. Something to get you from frozen to fluent without an inspirational quote or a 12-step plan to enlightenment that requires better lighting and looser yoga pants. Let's build it together. Quietly. Without fuss. One rung at a time.

In the first rung, the physical signals are the sign. Let's get one thing straight: that dry mouth? That flutter in your chest? That sense you've left the gas on in every house you've ever lived in? That's not failure. That's your elementary system reporting for duty.

It's the same system that would help you outrun a bear, were you ever unwise enough to holiday somewhere bears roam. It's just... *misassigned*. The bear this time is a deadline. Or a dinner. Or someone's disappointed sigh that lands like a slap. So, here's the shift: don't see it as panic. See it as data. Data means you can listen. And if you can listen, you can move.

To step up to the second rung, we can 'break and breathe twice'. *Thinking* won't save you here. Not yet. The mind's out of phase with the body when you're this wound up. So, we start simpler. Do something odd. Drop your pen. Tap your foot. Say a word you've not said since Year 8 geography. ('Archipelago' is oddly effective!)

Then breathe. Not deep—controlled. In for four. Hold for four. Out for four. Again. And again. You are not calming down. You are giving shape to chaos. The breath is not the fix. It's the invitation.

Now, check your tongue for the third rung. It's probably plastered to the roof of your mouth like it's hiding from a bomb scare. Let it go. Let it rest heavy and soft at the bottom of your mouth, like a cat draped over a radiator. That small shift will signal the jaw, neck, shoulders, breath—'stand down, troops'. This one isn't an attack.

On the fourth rung, you can begin to hum. Don't chant. Don't 'om'. Just hum for the fourth rung. Low. Soft. Like you're letting out a sound only the inside of your chest needs to hear. It will vibrate. That vibration will resonate as it speaks to your vagus nerve, that old friend of regulation, and it will say: 'All clear'. Three hums on the fourth rung. No audience. Just air and honesty.

As you step up to rung five, just think of a time—recent or ancient—when you felt competent and safe. Capable and safe. Steady. Grounded. *And close your eyes.*

Feel where it moved in your body. Did it move from your hands? In your tummy with your breath? The lift in your chest? Now, press thumb to your little finger. Or touch your chest, just at your heart—feel the beat... and the breath. *Link the gesture to the state.* Rehearse it. Repeat it. Next time the storm brews, you won't need to remember calm. You'll summon it to bring you home.

You can step on the sixth rung with ease: gently squeeze, as if you're holding in a pee, and count from three... two... one. And release. Let a deep sense of peace spread through your whole body—up to the top of your head, and down to your feet on the floor.

As pleasure and peace begin to increase, a message is sent deep into your core: now you are safe here, breathing and just drift. This feeling you feel is more than just calm. It's a sort of quiet bliss—a warm pleasure, soothing and kind. It is your body recalling what it feels like to soften.

The message is clear: here, you can *let go*. As you allow it to rise, you can begin to smile and something richer inside—something that feels like joy wrapped in sunlight, sparkling all over your skin. Now, let it seep deep within.

It lets you feel wonderful—from the tips of your toes to the back of your mind. It resets your whole system—your body, your breath, your mind and your skin; this time and next time.

Each time you repeat, the signal will strengthen. Take a sweet breath in; and squeeze and release, and let the sensation spread and increase. Let warmth flow from your heart, across your chest, all over your skin, into your mind and then down to your feet. You have been brought back to a joyful place, just for a spell: it's your natural self.

Hold onto this sense of warm belonging. The seventh rung is next and is calling. What is inside you will help you to rise.

As we move to rung seven, see yourself ten minutes after this storm has passed. Not triumphant. Just intact. Your shoulders are looser. Your face has softened. You're drinking tea or a sparkling drink. Taste it in your mind, feel your tongue, once more, on the seventh rung.

See yourself in your mind, calm, relaxed, safe and kind. It's your nervous system's breadcrumb trail back to composure. Borrow its breath. Steal its steadiness. Step into it like you own it—because you do.

The eighth rung tells you something new: the most capable people often spiral hardest. This time it was you. Next time, you'll catch it earlier, then earlier and earliest still. Because your mind and body will move as one to decompress sooner, faster and easier each time your body says: 'I need help.' And because you're reading this, you're already giving it.

And the song that is sung on the ninth rung is a pleasurable one. Because, once we've climbed out of the pit, we don't stop at boring, beige or neutral. Neutral is necessary, but it doesn't nourish you. Do something small and joyful. A scent. A song. A ridiculous dance behind closed doors. Joy isn't earned. It's wired in. And when you pair it with safety, your body remembers not just how to return to calm—but why it matters.

And in that flicker, it is your flame burning again. Beautiful, bright and kind. Lighting up your mind. On the tenth rung, you have fully come into where it is you need be. You don't need to be 'on' all the time. You can realise there's shiny new place, which was obscured, but you can now begin to see. We always need a way to get back online. So, make this yours:

Drop the tongue. Hum the breath. Anchor the capable. Squeeze and release. Picture the afterglow. Do it in the car. In the loo. In the lift. Between the 'send' and the 'reply'. You're not doing self care. You're issuing new instructions to a system that's always listened. You're giving it bigger buttons that are better buttons.

You're saying:

'I've got this. Even now... especially now.'

You don't need to be 'better'. You need to 'find home again'. Not instantly. Not perfectly. But on purpose. So, when or if the pit opens, and the floor drops out, and you feel your breath snag on the edge of self-doubt—just find that first rung. It's a simple signal for you to step onto next and drop your softened tongue.

For the rest of your life, even when you are weary, tired and old. My promise to you is that this ladder will hold. And now, FG, a quiet word about that itch in your thoughts. The one that says,

"But do I deserve to feel this good?"

It's faint at first. But you know its timbre. Reasonable. Familiar. Tightly tailored in the voice of your better judgement. It's the same voice that insists cake needs an occasion, joy needs a receipt, and calm must be earned in sweat and silence. This is not you being difficult. It's just a belief system that's been given tenure.

The story goes like this:

First prove you're not failing. Then, perhaps, you may rest. But only briefly. And joy? Joy is for those who've sorted the inbox of life.

Well, my dear FG, what if joy required no such clearance? What if joy is not the proof of a life well managed, but the signal that your system is finally clear enough to receive it? Let me put it another way: You don't need a reason to feel wonderful. You need a nervous system that's been shown how.

The old belief said: *If I relax now, I might miss something important.* The new belief is: *If I don't relax now, I'll miss everything important.*

The old belief said: *It would be irresponsible to feel good with so much undone.* The new belief is: *It is irresponsible to ignore what my system needs in order to get things done.*

The old belief said: *I'll feel calm when I deserve to.* The new belief is: *I will feel calm so I can remember who I am when I do.*

You see the pivot? You don't need a watertight justification for serenity. You need a physiology that can support it—and if beliefs that arrive that don't support it, boot them out the moment they arrive. You'll recognise them: they'll be wimpy and overdressed.

You've already done the hard part. You interrupted the spiral. You climbed back to breath. You surfaced to sensation. And now your system, that marvel of mammalian precision, is finally ready to experience something more radical than relief:

Joy. Wonder. Pleasure. Not as a treat. Not as a trickle-down dividend from a well-managed week. But as a basic mammalian right. Because here's the truth no one told you at school, and certainly not at that job where fatigue was mistaken for professionalism:

There is no virtue in the suffering that you no longer need.

You are allowed to feel brilliant without a single thing having improved on paper. You are allowed to feel peaceful while things still wobble. You are allowed, dear FG, to feel joy that arrives without an explanation and leaves you looking around wondering if it was meant for someone else. It was meant for *you*.

Let me offer you a few final thoughts to keep close when the old voices knock:

You don't need to be perfect to feel wonderful. You just need the access to that state. And you have it now. No oath required. No breakthrough necessary. No performance review from the gods.

Just this: the sense that your body is not under threat. That your breath is yours again. That something unnameable is beginning to stir —a warmth, a lift, a smile not meant for the public. Let it in. Let it stay.

And if the old beliefs tap on the window, let them watch. But don't let them in. They're not bad. Like spoiled food, they are out of date. Now? Now is a good moment to hum.

And maybe now, the question is no longer whether you're allowed to feel joy without justification. But simply whether your body is ready to remember how. And best of all? You won't need a reason. Just a nervous system that knows that:

Love, joy and pleasure are always in season.

P

TWO

THE CHANGING FACE OF RESILIENCE

DEAR P,

There was a time when I thought resilience meant holding my breath, just long enough to get through a difficult moment, the hard week, the overwhelming season. I believed that I could just grit my teeth and endure, then I'd earn the right to exhale on the other side. Resilience, back then, looked a lot like silence. Like pushing through without complaint, showing up even when I was too overwhelmed inside, and never admitting that I was struggling.

I wore exhaustion like a shield. I thought being strong meant not letting anything crack the surface. I'd keep moving, keep working, keep smiling – all while secretly counting the days until it would all quiet down. And when things finally settled, I wouldn't feel proud. I'd just feel empty. But I never questioned it. That was what I understood resilience to be: doing it all, carrying it all, and never asking for help.

A reel slipped into my timeline the other day. I wasn't looking for anything, but there it was – a woman talking about all the things she had worked for. And then she said something that made me think: *"I didn't feel proud or anything. There was no sense of accomplishment. Just... done. Like I was so over it. And I could finally breathe."*

It hit me because I've felt that too. That strange emptiness after the finish line, the silence after the storm you've been bracing yourself against. Not joy. Not pride. Just relief. And sometimes, not even that. Just a numb kind of stillness where you thought something meaningful would be.

There were days before that I couldn't even get myself to get up. I know I have work to do, reports to submit, messages to answer, things to check off – the usual. I was not sick, not in any obvious visible way. But my body felt heavy, like it's being held down by something invisible. I laid there, still, like every cell in me has decided it's had enough.

I told myself that I was just tired, that I'd reach out soon, but the truth is even the idea of conversation felt exhausting. I didn't know how to be around others too without pretending I was okay. So I avoided it altogether. The people who cared started to notice, but I brush them off with vague reassurances. "Just busy," I'd say. I couldn't find the energy to explain what I didn't fully understand myself.

When someone tried to offer help or even a gentle advice, I shut down. I'd nod politely, but inside, I rejected it, not out of pride but out of fear that accepting support meant admitting I wasn't okay. I didn't want to be seen that way. I thought if I kept my distance, I could keep control. But in trying to protect myself, I built a wall around everything. And that time I thought *"how lovely it would be to just disappear."*

Not permanently. Just for a while. To be suspended in nothingness where no one expects anything, where I don't have to perform, explain or pull myself together. A place where I'm not flooded by the guilt of not doing, the shame of needing rest, or the constant fear that I'm falling behind.

It's hard to admit that – the craving to vanish, even temporarily. Because we're told to keep going, to hustle, to show up no matter what. But what if the days I felt like I couldn't move weren't a sign of weakness but a message I've been too busy to hear? Maybe my body was asking for what my mind refused to allow – a pause, a boundary, a moment of grace.

That moment made me wonder how often we chase strength by way of self-abandonment, how often we treat resilience as something to survive rather than something that supports us. We power through. We deliver. We finish. But do we ever pause to ask *why* we keep carrying so much, or what it's costing us to appear strong?

Maybe resilience was never meant to be about bottling it all in. Maybe it's not about holding your breath until the pain passes, but learning to breathe through it, to stay open, even when things feel unbearably heavy. And maybe resilience, the way I'm learning it now is not about forcing movement when I feel stuck, but about listening to the stillness without shame.

Resilience used to mean holding everything in – swallowing the lump in my throat, ignoring the ache in my chest, and keeping my face composed no matter what was breaking inside. It meant showing up even when I was running on fumes, convincing everyone (including myself) that I was fine. I powered through long days, the disappointments, the loneliness. And when it got unbearable, I pushed even harder. Because that's what strong people did. That's what we were taught.

We admired those who never faltered, who carried the weight of the world without asking for help. But we rarely asked what it was doing to them on the inside. We didn't call it survival, we call it success. And so we wore exhaustion like a medal. We silenced our needs. We learned how to function while hurting, thinking that was strength. But more often than not, we weren't okay – we were just quiet.

Now, resilience looks different. It's softer, but no less powerful. It's recognising when I'm overwhelmed and saying so. It's learning to rest, not as a reward, but as a right. It's allowing emotions to move through me, not fearing that they'll make me weak. It's being honest about what I can't carry anymore and learning that putting something down is not the same as giving up.

There's something beautiful about this new kind of strength, the kind that doesn't shout or pretend. The kind that chooses healing over hiding. It's not about being unbreakable but being real. And in many ways, that version of resilience feels more radical and more freeing than anything we were ever taught before.

It's about making space for the good too. For so long, joy felt like something to be cautious of, as if it came with strings attached. I used to brace myself in moments of happiness, convinced it was only a matter of time before something went wrong. Like joy was a setup, and I needed to stay alert. But now, I'm learning that joy doesn't need to be earned. It can be safe. It can be whole.

I'm still learning, still unlearning. But with every breath I take without apologising for needing it, I feel more free. And maybe that's the point – to stop surviving our lives and start living them – fully, tenderly and without shame. I'm still figuring out what it means to be strong without being hard, and how to be soft without falling apart. Some days, I get it right. Other days, I had to stop myself consciously for going back to old habits, for bracing for the worst.

I'm still figuring it out, but I'm getting there.

Maybe there are better ways I haven't thought of yet. I'm sure you've found them. I wonder what it took for you to arrive there. Was it time? Was it loss? Or maybe it was a simple decision to stop proving and start being.

I'd love to hear how to live a life with more ease, more truth and more lightness, not just for myself, but so I can pass it to others too.

Until then,

FG

DEAR FG,

I read your letter with the kind of reverence usually reserved for old love letters found in library books or confessions mumbled during dental surgery—unintended, uncomfortable, and entirely too close to the nerve. What you wrote? That wasn't a letter. That was a slow exhale after years of holding your breath for applause that never came.

You wrote like someone who's finally realised the room's been on fire for years and now wonders why they're sweating. It was honest in a way that left no handrail—raw, sharp, and inconvenient. The kind of honesty most people avoid because it doesn't play well in meetings or over brunch.

And yes, I recognised every bloody word. Not because I'm noble or especially insightful, but because I've been there. More than once. The pit has a revolving door and excellent repeat business. I'm practically on a first-name basis with the echo.

You've done the hardest bit already—you named it. The weight, the stillness, the strange cocktail of exhaustion and dread that settles behind the eyes. Not dramatic enough to be tragic, not mild enough to be ignored. Just enough to make everything feel like effort. That middle place—where nothing's technically wrong, but everything feels subtly poisoned. Welcome to it.

What you call silence, the world often mistakes for strength. What you call stillness, they'll reward with extra responsibility. And what you call falling apart? Most people won't even notice. You'll just get compliments on how calm you seem while your internal monologue is playing a round of existential whack-a-mole.

So here we are. You wrote. I read. And now, against my better judgement, I'll reply. Not because I have solutions—God knows those are rarer than decent coffee in a staffroom—but because it would be rude not to.

Let's begin, shall we?

Ah yes—the pit. The emotional equivalent of being locked in a storage cupboard with all the lights off and your inner critic for company. You painted it well. The heaviness. The inertia masquerading as rest. The way every phone vibration feels like a summons from hell. That wasn't burnout, FG. That was your system staging a quiet mutiny, and you missed the pamphlet.

Everyone thinks the pit arrives with drama. A breakdown in a board-room. Tears in the middle of Woolies. A social media flounce. But more often, it creeps in wearing your calendar and your polite email signature. It whispers, 'You're fine, just tired.' And before you know it, your soul has been outsourced to Outlook, and your body's functioning on muscle memory and borrowed grace.

You called it silence. I'd call it operational shutdown with a friendly user interface. High-functioning despair. My personal favourite.

And when people offer help—bless them—you find yourself unable to reach back. Not because you're proud, but because accepting feels like stepping into a witness box: one more thing to survive. Besides, what would you even say? 'Hi, I'm drowning in plain sight, but I didn't want to be an inconvenience'?

So you retreat. Behind vagueness. Behind 'busy'. Behind digital presence and emotional absence. You wear performance like Kevlar and call it professionalism. And worst of all, they believe you. Because you're good at this. At appearing whole while quietly disassembling.

FG, if I had a *quid* for every time someone told me I seemed 'together' while I was googling existential therapists between meetings, I could afford to cry somewhere scenic.

So yes, you've been in the pit. No medals are handed out down there, but for what it's worth: I see you.

And you're not broken. Just brilliantly maladapted to a world that confuses productivity with worth and still thinks burnout is a personality trait.

People talk about recovery like it's a ladder. Clean, tidy, rung by rung. You fall, you rise. Simple. Efficient. Usually accompanied by an inspirational quote in a pastel font. But that's not how it works, is it? You don't climb your way out. You spiral. Sometimes sideways. Sometimes in circles. Occasionally backwards, wearing last week's emotions like yesterday's laundry. It's not pretty. It's not linear. It's not even particularly polite.

So here's the thing no one prints on mugs: the descent has a pattern. Not a neat one, but a recognisable one. It goes something like this.

First, something gives. Could be sudden—a catastrophic loss, a betrayal, a diagnosis. Or slow—erosion by expectation, performed strength, unsustainable belonging. Either way, the system buckles. The voice in your head that used to sound like you now sounds like a tax auditor with a God complex. Welcome to the descent.

Then comes the stillness. The shut-down. The moment you start replying 'fine' before they even ask. You're not lying, exactly. You're just no longer applying for rescue. The world becomes a muted radio station, and you're just static on a loop. Some call it burnout. Others, 'having a lot on'. I call it the freeze. Not because it's poetic, but because it's accurate. You're not living—you're buffering.

But then—somewhere in the midst of that suspended animation—a flicker. A twitch of humour. A remembered lyric. A scent, a sound, a stranger's kindness that cracks the shell. The system blinks. A spark. It's easy to miss. Especially if you've been training yourself to ignore softness. But it's there. The breath before the return.

And the return, FG, is rarely cinematic. No grand reveal. No sudden clarity. Just motion. Dull, ordinary, miraculous motion. You wash your hair. You feel the sun. You notice a laugh before it gets filed under inappropriate. You stop mistaking vigilance for virtue. That's it. That's the shape. A descent, a freeze, a spark, a return.

Nothing fancy. Just real. Practised. Human.

You didn't fall because you were weak. You fell because the cost of pretending not to was too high. And now? You're already moving again. You just needed someone to name it.

You were told to be strong. Which, in practice, meant quiet. Measured. Unbothered. A woman of substance who never spilled a drop. It's a tidy myth—strength as stoicism, resilience as uninterrupted productivity, dignity as emotional drought. Useful, of course. Especially to those who benefit from your uncomplaining competence.

But real strength? It's messier. Less photogenic. Often arrives wearing tracksuit bottoms and unwashed hair. It looks like saying 'no' without a 400-word apology. It looks like resting before you're shattered. It looks like feeling the thing instead of outsourcing it to your inbox or your diary.

That kind of strength won't get you promoted, but it will keep you human.

You mentioned softness. As if it were a flaw to be corrected. Let me tell you something that most leadership manuals wouldn't touch with a bargepole: *softness is advanced work*. It's easier to perform polished indifference than it is to admit you're tired. Easier to manage others' expectations than to let them see your need. Softness asks for presence. For boundary. For self-trust. And frankly, most people would rather buy another planner.

What they don't say is that every time you choose softness without collapse—when you feel something and stay standing—you're doing something most people spend their lives avoiding. You're telling your system: 'We can handle this. We can stay open.'

It's not the kind of thing that trends on LinkedIn. But it is the kind of thing that saves lives. Yours, most importantly.

You said you didn't want to disappear. You wanted a pause. A moment of grace. That's not selfish. That's sacred. Anyone who's ever clawed their way back from the brink knows that the real rebellion isn't to scream louder—it's to feel quietly, without explanation.

So yes. Be soft. Be wildly, precisely, unapologetically soft. It is the opposite of weakness. It is a bloody miracle.

Now, about joy.

It's a tricky bastard. Vanishes when chased. Shows up uninvited, usually when you're in the middle of something boring like doing the bins or boiling pasta. And when it does arrive, we tend to interrogate it like it's smuggling contraband. *Should I be this happy? Is this allowed? Have I earned it?* As if delight were some bureaucratic privilege requiring paperwork.

But here's the truth that polite society finds unsettling: joy is primitive. Immediate. Unreasonable. It doesn't ask permission, and it certainly doesn't require productivity as proof of worth. That's why it unnerves the well-adjusted. You can't monetise it. Can't KPI it. It's hard to sell a spreadsheet on wonder.

And yet—when it comes, you know. Everyone does. It lands the same way across ages, cultures, tax brackets. A flash of warmth in the chest. An exhale that feels like home. A laugh that surprises your throat. We each fall into grief in our own twisted, personalised ways—but joy? That arrives through the same door for all of us. Quiet. Bodied. True.

I think you're starting to feel it again. Not every day. Not in ticker-tape moments. But in flickers. Micro-saturations. That half-second when the world seems coloured in again—messy, imperfect, but finally alive. Maybe a smell, maybe a song. Maybe your own voice not sounding like a stranger. That's it. That's delight knocking politely on the door of your nervous system, asking if it might come in and stay for a spell.

You don't need to justify it. You certainly don't need to delay it. Let it in. Even if it feels premature. Even if you're still wearing grief like a borrowed coat. Joy isn't waiting for you to be fixed. It just needs you to be available.

So where does that leave us?

Not at a resolution. Don't trust those. They're for Hallmark cards and personal development seminars with terrible catering. What you've got now isn't closure—it's motion. Slight, stubborn, entirely sufficient. You're moving again. Not back, and not up. Just forward, which is the only direction the body actually understands.

You don't need to do anything heroic next. No grand reinventions. No redemption arcs. No public declarations involving sunrise yoga or 'finally finding your voice'. Please. Spare us both. Just keep choosing not to disappear. Keep letting the breath arrive. Let the joy be silly, and let the silence be soft, not strategic.

And on days when the spiral dips again—as it will—you'll know the map better. You won't panic at the stillness. You'll remember: this is just the bit between the twitch and the turn. Nothing's wrong. The system is just catching its breath.

You're not late. You're not broken. You're not behind. You're simply coming back online. On your own terms. At your own damn pace.

That's the real work, FG. Not the performative resilience. Not the curated vulnerability. Just this—this precise and ordinary courage: to feel something and stay.

And yes, I'm in your corner. Grudgingly. Not waving a banner, but maybe holding snacks. No hugs—unless strictly necessary, and even then, we'll blame the weather.

Yours in slow return,

P

THREE
WHEN INNER VOICES SPEAK LOUDER

DEAR P,

I just remembered back when I was still working in corporate. It was one of those seasons where I felt confident in my role. I wasn't managing a team or heading a department, but I had a solid handle on things and my then supervisor seemed to notice. I'd often be asked to guide trainees or let them shadow me, not because it was my job, but perhaps because they trusted how I do things.

That kind of trust has its own weight though. There's this certain feeling of pride that comes when others start to see you as capable. I remember feeling calm and sure, almost like I settled into my own rhythm.

There was something steady about those days. I'd have my coffee tumbler in hand, headphones on the other then go over the mental list of things to check before getting started. Without anyone needing much to say, someone new would be assigned to sit beside me, watch how I navigate the systems or ask me questions in between tasks. I liked it. I liked being someone people could quietly rely on. It felt really good to be trusted for how I carried things.

It's a rare kind of joy – when your work becomes something others want to model. It's not because you're the best, but because there's something in the way you move that makes others believe they can do it too. Looking back now, it was one of the grounding seasons of my professional life. It's just steady and full of those small, subtle smiles that said, 'you're doing well... keep going.'

And then, somewhere in the middle of all that steadiness, I slipped.

It wasn't a huge thing. I'd given a trainee a piece of information that, in that moment, I was sure about. I'd explained it confidently, like I'd done so many times before. But a few hours later, while double-checking something else, I realised I'd gotten it wrong. Just a tiny detail. One line in a process. Nothing that could derail anything. But still – it was wrong.

Later in the afternoon, I got called in by my supervisor. Not for a warning or a serious talk – just for a casual conversation that subtly involved the correct process of things. A refresher, they said. They learned about the step I explained that wasn't quite aligned with the updated process.

No complaints were raised. The trainee hadn't even flagged it. And my supervisor was kind about it, clear but not stern. It wasn't a reprimand. If anything, it was the gentlest kind of course correction. But as I sat there nodding and thanking them for the reminder, something shifted within me.

It was a shift in how I began to see myself. I replayed the interaction in my head more times than I care to admit. That grounded confidence I'd been walking in? It began to feel like something fragile, with just a nudge it can crumble. A small voice surfaced: *Maybe they trusted the wrong person?*

Sadly, it echoed. It didn't make sense. I knew I'd made the mistake out of an honest slip, a misstep, like anyone could have. But the more I thought about it, the more the voice grew louder. Every time I reflected on the situation, I heard the same voice: *What if you're not as capable as you think?*

What was strange was that everything went back to normal. No one made a big deal out of it. Yet, there I was, caught in a storm of doubt. It left me questioning not just my ability to explain processes, but my entire sense of self in that role. What was happening?

I began to see how this voice, the inner critic, was shaping my reality. It wasn't loud but its consistent presence affected everything I did. It told me to second-guess my actions, to overthink my words. I noticed a shift in how I approach my work – more hesitation, more checking and rechecking, less confidence.

It took me a while to realise that this voice wasn't an objective truth. It wasn't the reality of my capabilities, but a reflection of an old belief trying to resurface. The more I listened to it, the more I doubted myself. But once I acknowledged it for what it was – just a thought, not fact, I found a way to move beyond it.

I wonder if there's others like me who let their inner voices shape their reality. Do they easily dodge those voices and move on, or do they struggle with them just as I did?

I've learned over time, that trusting the process is just as important as trusting myself. That errors made, no matter how simple they are, doesn't mean failing. I've learned to appreciate more the concept of learning and winning. Although I'm still curious. What's your take on this? How do you quiet the voice of doubt when it starts to shape your reality?

All the best,

FG

My Dear FG,

You know, I was just sitting here reflecting on the various ways we self-destruct with style—when your letter arrived, perfectly timed, like a tiny grenade in a velvet envelope. And what a letter it was. You described, with unnerving elegance, how one forgettable hiccup in a generally unremarkable day became an existential reckoning. Impressive, really. Most people need a crisis. You managed it with a *procedural misstep*.

You were doing well. In rhythm. In flow. Tumbler in hand, headphones in place, confidence humming along like a well-oiled espresso machine. Then—one incorrect instruction. One line. That's all it took. A ripple in the matrix. And boom: suddenly you're questioning your worth like someone found the wrong date on your birth certificate.

Now, to be clear: what you described isn't unusual. It's *alarmingly common*. But your mistake wasn't in the detail. It was in the aftermath: the court you summoned inside your own head, and the trial you conducted without witnesses, evidence, or snacks.

Before we go any further, let me offer some comparative relief. Because perspective is a gift. And you, my friend, are long overdue.

Let's begin with a man who demanded a *pubic* apology: he meant 'public', of course. He just didn't type it that way. And rather than quietly noticing and correcting it—perhaps with a cup of tea and a quiet moment of horror—he sent it. Company-wide. In bold. Underlined. Subject line: *Urgent Behavioural Breach*. Legal saw it. HR saw it. The receptionist saw it twice because she printed it by accident.

And still, rather than perishing from shame or changing his name and moving to a cave, this man was later promoted. You see, *pubic apology* became a firm legend. A ritual, even. People would whisper it at leaving drinks. 'Go on, give us a pubic apology.' And laugh.

Because everyone knew what it meant: *you survived the worst and still had the keys to your office.*

Next up, the case of 'PowerPoint Treason'. Brent was smooth and suave. The kind of man whose cufflinks had monograms and whose metaphors had footnotes. He had a universal deck—one slide show to rule them all! Swap the logo, change the footer, and off you go.

Except one fateful Thursday, he clicked through Slide 17, mid-pitch, to a client he called their 'greatest strategic ally'. And there it was: *the competitor's logo.* Front and centre.

Celebrated. Annotated. Colour-coded. He stared at it. The client stared at it. The intern took a screenshot!

And what did he do? He smiled. He gestured. And said:

'And as you can see, even your rivals aspire to this calibre of collaboration'.

He wasn't fired. He was promoted. Because some people don't bluff. They *transcend.*

And finally, we come to a high-flyer I call, 'The Crimson Avenger'. Smart. Persuasive. Composed—until he wasn't. Anger made him flush. Embarrassment made him blush. Not subtly. He turned the colour of raw steak left out in the sun. The more he argued, the redder he became. Clients stopped listening to the words and started scanning the room for available medical equipment.

We once watched him deliver a devastating line in a contract negotiation, only to be offered a glass of water and a seat near the air con. It was difficult to win an argument when your face kept suggesting imminent cardiac arrest. And yet—he went on to lead one of the most profitable divisions in the company. Because *performance doesn't care about your blood pressure's sense of drama.*

Let's now revisit your catastrophe. You gave a trainee a slightly incorrect procedural detail. A single line. A pebble on the footpath. No full-company email. No rogue logos. No thermonuclear blushing. Just a slip, noted and gently corrected. And yet—your inner voice grabbed that pebble, put it on a velvet cushion, lit it with a spotlight and asked if anyone else wanted to come and see the fraud in action.

Let's apply the *4Cs of Believing* to sequence:

- *Cause*: You slipped.
- *Consequence*: Mild correction.
- *Criteria*: You must never be wrong.
- *Conclusion*: You're a fraud.

That's not just unfair. That's a *rigged system*. In one case, it took months to build your self-trust. In the other, it took seconds to blow it up. That's the cost of having perfection as your benchmark: anything less becomes disqualifying. So, let's rewind and apply the 4Cs again —this time to your pre-collapse confidence. Because here's what's truly astonishing: how differently you evaluated the same person— you.

As for that self-belief you were walking around with before? It wasn't made of fluff. It was *systematically constructed*:

- *Cause*: You showed up, reliably.
- *Consequence*: People trusted you.
- *Criteria*: Consistency, composure, capability.
- *Conclusion*: You were grounded. Confident. Trustworthy.

That's evidence-based leadership. That's earned assurance. But when you made a single, small, deeply human mistake, you applied a *different system entirely*. A system where the *criteria* silently shifted from 'competent over time' to 'flawless in every instant'. From 'respected by peers' to 'omniscient or else'. That's not just irrational. That's a theological standard.

And forgive me, but unless you've been quietly performing miracles between meetings, I'm fairly sure you're just human. You breathe air, not prophecy. You trip occasionally. You correct course. You learn. And that is not a flaw—it's the contract.

So, if you've been applying divine standards to your all-too-mortal performance, it might be time to revise the terms and conditions. The ones that say you're only valuable if you never err? *Shred them*. They're written in vanishing ink anyway.

Let me put it plainly: the problem isn't that you slipped. It's that you thought slipping made you unworthy of trust. But the trust wasn't built on your infallibility. It was built on your steadiness, your rhythm... your *reliability*. And all of that remains. One line can't undo it.

You were embarrassed. Fair. But embarrassment, like anger, fear and sadness, is simply what happens when the body tries to turn a mole-hill into a mountain. Wisdom is what brings us back down, preferably with a cup of tea and a laugh at our own expense.

So, what now? You carry on. You restore your rhythm. You nod at the inner critic when it appears... but stop letting it hold the remote. You remember that moral leadership isn't just how you treat others when they fail—it's also how you treat *yourself* when you do. Next time that voice rises—disapproving and terribly persuasive—ask yourself:

'Would I say this to someone I care about? Would I let someone else speak to me like this?'

If not, then don't allow it from someone wearing your voice.

And finally, remember this: every legend begins with something awkward. A misstep. A misplaced logo. A face the colour of chilli paste. And yet, we endure. We rise. We get better at laughing sooner. That, my dear FG, is what leadership feels like on the inside.

Write soon. Preferably before the critic drafts your resignation.

Yours, with mild mockery and real respect,

P.

FOUR
FINDING STILLNESS IN CHAOS

MY TRUSTED CONFIDANT,

Life has a funny way of pushing us to the edge, just to see if we'll wobble.

There have been moments before when I felt unstoppable—like I could take on anything the world threw at me. Then, in the blink of an eye, it all changes. My mind went blank, my body frozen, and my heartbeat pounded so loudly that I could literally hear it.

Imagine dropping a mentos to a bottle of Coca Cola. There was stillness at first and then... boom! Thoughts fizzed, overflowed then scattered. My brain was suddenly in full panic mode, desperately trying to put the cap back on before things got any messier.

Stress has a way of sneaking up to me like that—one moment, I was cool and collected; the next, I was a shaken-up bottle ready to explode.

I always thought the question was, "How do I stop feeling stressed?"—as if the goal was to eliminate stress entirely. But let's be real, life will always find new ways to shake the bottle. So instead, I revised the question to *"How do I train myself to remain calm in chaos?"*

I've come to realise that stress isn't something we can simply delete from our lives—it's wired into us for a reason. But what we can do is train our brains to react differently. You always say that when you think different, you'll feel differently and eventually you'll act differently. That really stuck with me.

It made me think that calming the mind isn't only about deep breaths and positive affirmations—it starts with how we think about stress itself. If I see stress as an enemy, something to fight against, it only makes the pressure worse. But if I reframe it as a signal, a challenge, or even a tool, suddenly, I have more control.

I used to have this bad habit of bottling everything up until I inevitably explode. At first, I'd tell myself, "It's fine. It'll be over soon." I'd push through, convinced that it'll just pass. I thought that if I just kept everything under control, that if I just kept going, that if I just hold my breath a little longer and powered through – it would eventually go away.

But stress just won't disappear. It built and built and built. It stayed and lingered, very much unwelcomed. Every little frustration, every worry and unspoken thought added to the pressure. And since I wasn't releasing any of it, the pressure had only one way to escape and that's all at once, in a big messy explosion.

I'd snap over something trivial – a misplaced phone, a slow internet connection, someone asking a simple question at the wrong time. And that's when it dawned on me that it wasn't just those small, silly things. It was because of everything I've been holding in.

I thought that bottling things meant I was being strong. But the reality is, it was making me even more fragile – always one shake away from bursting.

It took me a long time and a few trances to realise that that approach wasn't working. Stress wasn't the enemy, my inability to handle it was. You actually helped me see a pattern. The more I ignored stress, the worse it became. And the more I bottled things up, the bigger the eventual explosion.

That's when it finally hit me. Instead of feeling like an over-shaken soda bottle about to burst, I learned that the trick is to release the pressure in controlled bursts. It's loosening the cap just enough to let the excess air out without making a mess. I became more attune with myself by recognising when the stress or pressure is rising and responding in way that's steady and calm.

I've learned that handling stress isn't about suppressing everything or letting it be until it is no longer chaotic, it's about finding stillness within it.

Warmly,

F.G.

My Young Friend,

What a letter. What a leap.

You've moved from wondering about mindfulness to *embodying* it under fire—and in doing so, you've crossed an invisible but momentous threshold.

The tone of your writing has changed. It no longer gropes for understanding like someone fumbling for a light switch. It offers understanding—like someone who's struck a match in the dark and begun to see.

Your Mentos-in-Coke metaphor was vivid and dangerously accurate. I could feel the fizz in my chest. That's how insight often arrives: not in neat graphs, but in carbonated chaos. Not clean. Not tidy. But kinetic.

And it's clear you've grasped something many spend decades trying to avoid—stress isn't the enemy. It's not failure, and it's not flaw. It's a message. And like most messengers, it keeps knocking louder until we answer the door.

You asked:

"How do I train myself to remain calm in chaos?"

Then, in the very next breath—you answered. You're loosening the cap. Releasing pressure in deliberate bursts. That's not theory. That's wisdom with dirt under its nails. That's what resilience looks like.

Not *clench and endure,* but *know your threshold and breathe.*

And this line of yours stopped me:

"I thought that bottling things meant I was being strong. But the reality is, it was making me even more fragile."

There it is. The paradox no one wants printed on a coffee mug:

Real strength isn't how tightly you can hold on.

It's how skilfully you let go.

That's what I meant when I wrote:

> *To soften is to conquer stress.*

Not collapse. Not give in. But release the white-knuckled grip so you can move *with* the storm, not against it. And here's the part you're beginning to live into:

> Joy isn't a reward for being strong.
> It's your birthright—chaos and all.

Your evolving response to stress reminds me of a truth that took me years to believe:

> *We can't cancel chaos.*
> *But we can cultivate stillness that moves with it.*

And this stillness—true stillness—isn't silence. It's *space*. Not the absence of noise, but the presence of room to move, room to breathe. And from what I see, you're starting to find that room. Even as the walls shake.

May I offer a small practice in that spirit? One that doesn't promise transformation—just traction.

Pause. Soften. Savour. Breathe.

Whenever the fizz starts rising—when your breath shortens or your jaw braces—pause. Not for long. Just long enough to:

- *Soften.* Drop your shoulders. Let your tongue settle on the floor of your mouth.
- *Savour.* Look for one thing—anything—neutral or beautiful. A patch of light. A colour. A shadow.
- *Breathe.* Three slow breaths, while staying with what you saw.

Do it not to fix. But to return. To re-enter yourself. Because what you're learning now is this:

> *Stress isn't a bomb to defuse. It's a tide to watch.*

And the more often you practise presence in motion, the more often you'll find joy—not the fireworks kind, but the kind that waits patiently beneath the foam. Let me end, fittingly, with your words:

> "Finding stillness within it"

That's not just poetry. That's a nervous system re-learning its birthright. And what you've described—Not stillness *after* the storm, but stillness *inside* it—That's where beauty begins to live.

Not as an idea, but as a felt presence. That is the heartbeat of *amouria.* Whether named or not.

Write soon,

P

FIVE
THE "WHAT IF" LOOP: A MEMORY ON REPEAT

DEAR P,

The past has a way of quietly clinging to us. Sometimes it returns as a sharp pang, other times a soft ache in an ordinary day. A scent, a street corner, an old building, a line from a song – and suddenly we're back in a moment we thought we'd forgotten. We feel the weight of what was said, or wasn't. We imagine different endings, rewrite the scenes, wonder what might have been if we had just done it differently. It's strange how memories can still stir something deep.

I didn't think much of it then, but I remember how my grandmother always held me, not by the hand, but firmly by the wrist – whenever we went out or crossed the street. I must've been around four or five. I would fidget and twist away, trying to wriggle my wrist free, or sometimes reach up to hold her hand instead, not understanding why she wouldn't let me choose. She'd gently scold me, and I'd sulk, unaware of the worry behind her grip. Back then, it just felt like a restriction. It wasn't until years later, long after her hands had grown still, that I realised what that hold truly meant – and how some moments, small as they are, anchor themselves in us long after we've left them behind.

I've lost count of how many times I've played the "if only" game in my head. If only I had held on tighter. If only I could go back – not to change anything, but just to be in that moment again. Just to feel what it was like to be protected so completely, so instinctively before I even understood the dangers of the world. In a few years I had with her, she gave me more than I ever realised at that time. She was simply "Mama Taty" for me – warm, dependable, always there. The one who walked me to kindergarten, who warmed water in the kettle so I could bathe in comfort. The one who taught me prayers in our mother tongue, made sure I ate healthy lunches, and always bought little treats whenever we stopped by 7-Eleven. She gifted me barbies and toy soldiers alike – quietly breaking gender norms before I even knew what they were. And every time I came home for a visit, there would always be chocolates waiting – set aside just for me.

I knew her in the familiar ways a child knows love – in small routines, gentle gestures and every day acts of care. But later, I came to learn that she was so much more to others. A teacher. A principal. A leader in her own right. People speak of her with reverence, of how she shaped lives beyond our home. And yet, even knowing all that, what stays with me the most are the ways she shaped *mine*, in the every day moments no one else saw.

I was around twelve when she passed and for years after that, I remember praying over and over – begging, really – for her to appear in my dreams. Even just once. Just to see her again, to feel her presence, to say the things I didn't get to say. But she never came. And maybe that absence, the silence of it, was what made me cling harder to the memories. I got stuck there. In the what-ifs. In the aching wish to have one more day, one more hour. Not to relive everything, just to *stay*, just to be in her presence again.

Sometimes I imagine how things could've been different if she were still here. If I could've taken care of her the way she once cared for me. If I could've said thank you – for shielding me from people who meant harm, for the strength she passed on when I didn't even know I'd need it. These thoughts didn't come gently. They arrive like waves, or sometimes like flashes – mid-conversation, mid-errand, mid-silence. In my head, I played our story past its real ending. I kept writing scenes that never happened. I imagined her witnessing my life now, her pride, her gentle correction, her laughter.

The memory played like a movie I never stopped directing. Sometimes grainy and slow, other times vivid and loud. Certain moments returned on cue – as if my heart had internal seasons where grief bloomed all over again. I've come to accept that there are people whose love becomes part of your wiring. You don't get over them. You carry them forward.

And yet, there's something about memory that isn't always kind. The sweet ones, like mama Taty holding my wrist, feel like warm sunlight, but the painful ones? They linger like shadows. And more often than not, it's the ones filled with pain, betrayal, anger, or injustice that refuse to leave. We replay them in our minds, analysing every word said, every action done, every wound that never got its apology. As if going over it one more time will give us closure. But all it really does is keep the wound fresh – bleeding beneath the surface, invisible to others but heavy in the chest.

I've noticed how we carry these moments – clutching them like stones in our pockets. We think we've moved on, but they weigh us down in ways we don't always recognise. They show up in how we mistrust others, in how we overreact, in how we shrink from things that remind us of what once hurt. Even when no one else can see it, we're still living in defense of a past that already happened. It's like our nervous system doesn't forget, even when our mind tries to.

And there was a strange kind of comfort in that pain, isn't there? As twisted as it sounds, sometimes staying angry feels safer than being vulnerable again. Holding on to the injustice gives us a sense of control, like we're protecting ourselves from ever being caught off guard. But the longer we grip it, the more it grips us. We stop being who we are now – and instead, we become keepers of old hurt, archivists of wounds. We not only remember the past, we also start reliving it, sometimes daily.

I think that's the real trap of the "what ifs" – not just the longing, but the idea that the past *owes* us something. A different ending. An apology. A redo. But the past is stubborn. It won't rewrite itself, no matter how many times we revisit it. And until we decide to stop bargaining with what was, we'll always be stuck in between – half here, half there. Half healed, half haunted.

In one of the conversations we had, you asked me a question that stopped me cold: *"Who benefits from ruminating on these things – especially the awful ones?"* And I remember sitting with that. Because the truth is... no one does. The people who hurt us? They've likely moved on. The moment that wounded us? It's long gone. The past is done. It's over. And yet, here we still are – still standing at its doorstep, hoping that if we knock long enough, we'll get something different. But we won't. What we get is delay. Distraction. The ache of a life half-lived.

And that's the cost, isn't it? Staying in that cycle, spinning the reel of what was, and what should've been, only keeps us from living the life that we *actually* want. A life that's not built in reaction to pain, but in alignment with possibility. But that kind of life can't be lived while we're still tied to old battles. We can't move forward with our hands clenched around the past.

That's where regret quietly slips in. It's like a whisper we can't unhear. It wraps itself around the what ifs, feeding the loop. And the more we replay those moments, the more real they feel until we start confusing memory with truth. It fixates on the version of us that didn't know better yet.

And the more we let regret narrate our days, the more we begin to fear the future too. We stop trusting our decisions. We second-guess our instincts. We hesitate to try again – because the memory of getting it wrong becomes louder than our desire to get it right. Regret tells us not to reach, not to take risks. It convinces us that we've already lost too much, and that trying again will only hurt more. So we stall. And somewhere along the way, we confuse that shutdown state with safety.

It is up to us to decide and stop it from taking charge. We can acknowledge regret without being consumed by it. We can say, *"Yes, that hurt. But I'm still allowed to move forward and not get stuck. I'm allowed to become someone better."* Because we can't edit the past, but we can choose what we carry from it. We are allowed to imagine a future not shaped by our shame, but by our courage to begin again.

So thank you P, for teaching me that letting go is not about forgetting, but refusing to let it run the show. That remembering doesn't have to mean reliving but honouring the good ones. That I can carry love without carrying the pain. That I can honour the past without being held hostage by it.

And now, as I write this, older and a little wiser – I'm finally learning how to hold my wrist in the same way my grandma held it. With firmness. With care. With so much love. With the understanding that while I can't rewrite the past, I can choose not to let it write *me*. I can now pause the mental replay, step out of the story loop, and be fully present. I can remind myself that the life I long for doesn't live behind me. It lives here. In presence. In peace. In choosing not to carry what no longer needs to come with me.

And if I forget, I have this memory – of a wrist, gently but firmly held. Of a love that anchored me even when I didn't understand it.

I didn't expect that a memory so small could hold so much. But looking back now, I see how these seemingly ordinary moments become symbols, anchors, and mirrors. And through our conversations, I've started to see that letting go isn't loss. It's liberation. We're not meant to live backwards. That peace comes not from rewriting the past, but from rewriting our relationship to it. Again, thank you, for holding space for this story, for helping me loosen my grip and for reminding me where life really lives.

Not in the rerun, but in the choosing – right here, right now, with both feet in today.

With light and gratitude,

FG

FG,

There are memories that sit politely on a shelf, yellowing with time. And then there are the others — the ones that crouch behind your ribs and pounce at unexpected moments. Yours — the wrist, the dream that wouldn't arrive, the loop that played like it had something urgent to say — that's the second kind. The kind that never quite announces itself yet insists on being answered. What you wrote didn't read like a letter. It read like a gentle exorcism.

You didn't tell me about your grandmother. You summoned her. Not in grand gestures or funeral eulogies, but in the scalded kettle, the wrist-grip, the bloody *Barbies* and soldiers on the same plastic battle-field. What a woman. What a curriculum. Most people get gender roles stuffed down their throats; you got them deconstructed in a 7-Eleven snack aisle, served with chocolates and a side of maternal vigilance.

And yet for all that reverence — for all the light you cast her in — there was one haunting absence that slipped between your lines. She never came back. Not in the dream. Not once. That empty stage you kept lit night after night, just in case she returned for a curtain call — stayed quiet. And still you held on.

The grip became yours. What began as her hand on your wrist hard-ened into your own fist — around grief, guilt, and a perfectly rational desire to change the unchangeable. You weren't holding on to her. You were holding on to *what didn't happen.*

That's the clever part about memory. It doesn't just preserve what was. It polishes what wasn't until it gleams like truth. It rewinds the tape but swaps the script. And no one tells you how much it costs — to keep playing director in a film that's already wrapped.

You said the moments returned on cue. That your body seemed to have internal seasons of grief. That's not madness. That's pattern. Some call it trauma. Others call it winter. Either way, the result is the same: the body keeps score, but no one tells you what game you're playing.

So yes — I see you. Not just in your eloquence, but in your exhaustion. Not just in your reverence for Mama Taty, but in the raw ache of someone who loved deeply and lost silently. And in case no one else has said it, I will: there's nothing weak about wanting one more hour. Nor is it foolish to wish that a dream might carry the weight of unfinished love.

But the game's rigged. The past doesn't answer, no matter how many times you knock. It doesn't even leave the porch light on. So maybe the real question isn't:

'Why hasn't she come back?'

Maybe it's:

'What if you've been carrying her forward all along?'

And maybe that firm grip — the one you now hold over your own wrist — isn't a shackle. Maybe it's a signal. And maybe it's time to let your hand go. Not because the story ends here. But because the next chapter is waiting. And it's impatient. Let this, then, be the moment we turn the page.

The dead don't need your suffering. They don't need you frozen midstep, carrying old scenes like unpaid debts. They don't require annual tributes of tears or the slow bleed of paralysing guilt. What they require—if anything at all—is that you bloody well live. Not just survive. *Live.* With your back straight, your voice clear, and your wrist no longer feeling gripped by ghosts demanding tribute they never asked for.

The highest form of remembrance isn't silence. It's motion. It's presence. It's becoming the person they hoped you'd be—not by performing grief, but by participating in life.

She held your wrist, yes—but not as a prison guard. Not to bind you to trauma. She was keeping you safe from traffic. That grip? Instinct. Her version of a seatbelt. The moment the danger passed, she let go. Because she trusted you'd learn to cross streets on your own.

But your body didn't get the memo. It held on. It turned protection into pattern. The grip became a rule. You weren't being shielded anymore—you were being haunted. And here's the trick: the memory doesn't do the haunting. You do—by replaying what never got to end cleanly.

Pain arrives loud, like a siren. But if it stays too long, it morphs into habit. And we keep stroking the wound, thinking it honours the love. It doesn't. It just means we haven't yet learned the difference between memory and self-harm.

Memory isn't the enemy. It's not the jailor. It's the bookshelf. You decide what's referenced, what's shelved, what gets quietly retired. That's not erasure. That's curation. You're not deleting her. You're deciding what parts of her to live forward.

Somatic grief—the ache in the wrist, the way your body flinches at familiar places—that's not a curse. It's a signal. But signals are meant to be *noticed*, not inhabited. If you rehearse loss, your nervous system will keep cueing it up. Not out of cruelty—but because it thinks that's the job.

You stayed loyal to pain because it felt like the last thread that tied you to her. But loyalty isn't the same as legacy. Legacy asks, "What next?"

You're not a broken heirloom. You're the continuation. And regret? That sneaky bastard—sells itself as wisdom but delivers paralysis. If it were useful, you'd feel lighter by now. But you don't. You feel stalled. Because regret doesn't protect you from pain—it just rehearses failure until the future starts to look suspect.

Let's call rumination what it is: a loop. It feels like work, but it's just emotional cardio. You're not searching for truth—you're chasing a different ending. But endings don't change. *Meaning does.* And meaning belongs to you. So, stop being the archivist of pain. Be the *author of continuation*. Not because the wound didn't matter. But because it doesn't get to write your next chapter. Closure isn't given. It's created. Not in silence or explanation—but in *motion*.

If you're waiting for the past to apologise, you'll wait forever. The dead don't send postcards. But they do leave blueprints—values, gestures, the warmth of hands that once held yours. That's enough.

She didn't return in dreams because she never left daylight. She lives in the grip you now offer others. In the early warnings, in the tiny acts of care. You're fluent in her handwriting, even if you're still looking for her signature.

Let the risk of presence be your tribute. Let your breath—this one and the next—be your offering. Let your smallest kindnesses be her love extended through time. Let the wrist you hold now be not from fear, but reverence.Because it's not the loss that defines you. It's who you become *after*.

You waited for her in your dreams. Night after night, your mind left the porch light on. Hoping she'd wander back through the dark with some last word. One more look. A nod. Something tidy to round off what real life had left ragged. But she never showed. And I can almost hear your heartbreak limping around behind that silence, as if you'd been stood up by someone who promised to haunt you faithfully.

Here's the part no one tells you: some people don't come back in dreams because they've already moved in somewhere better. She didn't return in your sleep because she never left your daylight. She reappeared in the firmness with which you now hold your own wrist. In the way you notice danger early. In the little acts of care you offer others before they even realise they need them. You're still waiting for her signature — but you're already fluent in her handwriting.

Those chocolates? You buy them now for other people. The kettle she warmed? You light stoves now for those freezing in shame. She taught you prayers. You turned them into presence. Not everyone needs incense and Latin for legacy. Sometimes a decent lunch and eye contact will do.

And yes, she gave you barbies and soldiers — which was less a shopping decision than a quiet revolution. A woman who understood, long before it was trendy, that love isn't about correcting the child. It's about expanding the world they believe they belong in. You belong everywhere now. She made sure of that. The door's open. The grip is gone. The world has been handed to you with both hands.

So, if you're still waiting for her to show up, I'll say this gently: she already did. You're just standing so close to the flame, you didn't realise you were the lantern. There's no need for another dream. *You* are the dream.

You don't need to rehearse pain to prove that it mattered. You lived it. You learnt it. You carry the lesson without needing to keep licking the wound. So, here's a permission slip — not that you need one.

- You're allowed to step out of the rerun.
- You're allowed to stop guarding the ashes.
- You're allowed to walk forward with both hands free.

And if anyone asks what you're doing? Tell them:

'I'm continuing her story, not repeating it.'

With less grip, more grace,

P

INTERLUDE—THE BODY REMEMBERS DIFFERENTLY

Not in years or sentences, but in weight and weather.

Some days, grief rises like steam—

soft, unsummoned, curling at the edges of breath.

Other days it is bone—

quiet, exacting, and entirely unmoved by reason.

But here's what we forget:

You are not obligated to make sense of your sadness

before it's allowed to leave.

Sometimes, what lingers isn't the story.

It's the muscle that learned to brace without permission.

So—uncurl. Unclench. Unname it, if you must.

What mattered was never what slipped away.

It's what stayed to keep you whole.

SIX
SMALL HABITS. BIG IMPACT.

DEAR P,

I trust life has been kind to you.

Lately, I've been reflecting on how small, seemingly insignificant changes can shape our lives in profound ways. It's easy to believe that transformation requires grand, sweeping actions—quitting a job, moving across the world, or reinventing ourselves overnight. But I'm beginning to wonder if the most meaningful changes come from something quieter: the tiny, consistent habits we weave into our days.

One memory keeps returning to me. When I was a child, I didn't enjoy reading. Books felt like a chore—something I had to do for school, not something I wanted for myself. My mom never pushed me. Instead, she'd bring home library books and leave them on the table. At first, I ignored them. But as the stack quietly grew, so did my curiosity. One day, I picked up a book—not to read it, but just to flip through a few pages. One page turned into two, then three. Before I knew it, I'd finished the book—without even realising I was reading.

That small moment changed everything. No big decision. Just a click in my brain. *One small shift.*

It's subtle, but lasting. Reading stopped feeling like an obligation and became something natural, even enjoyable. I started reaching for books on my own—not because I had to, but because I wanted to. And it's made me wonder: how many other areas of life could be transformed by small, consistent actions like that?

In the recent weeks, I've been exploring mindfulness in that same spirit. Not in any formal or structured way—just little moments of attention. A pause before replying. A slow breath while waiting for site pages to load. Noticing how my feet feel in my shoes. Listening intently during a conversation instead of just waiting for my turn to speak. It's surprising how even these brief pauses can shift my perspective, if only slightly. I'm still finding my way with it, and I'd love your thoughts. How do you approach mindfulness in your own life? Are there particular practices or habits that have helped you deepen your awareness?

I've also been thinking about patience. It's easy to get excited about a new habit or idea, only to feel disheartened when the results aren't immediate. But I'm starting to see that meaningful change often unfolds slowly, like a flower blooming in its own time. It's not about dramatic leaps, but about staying consistent—even when progress is invisible. How do you maintain patience and persistence when working toward long-term goals? Do you think there's room for both small steps and bold leaps, or do you find one more reliable than the other?

Thank you, as always, for being someone I can turn to with these thoughts. Your wisdom means so much to me, and I'm eager to hear your perspective.

Warmly,

FG.

My Young Friend,

Your letter arrived like a cool breeze on a hot day—welcome and well timed. It invited reflection, not only on your words, but on the quiet, often invisible way small, deliberate actions accumulate into something profound. You've touched on a truth most people overlook in the age of productivity porn and overnight transformations: the quiet rhythm of repeated intention is what actually reshapes us. Not the dramatic leap, but the hundred quiet lunges.

Your story—how a reluctant child became, almost by accident, a reader—is more than charming; it's strategic. It reveals a principle lost on most improvement junkies: habits grow best not under pressure, but in proximity. A book on the table is not a demand—it's a nudge wearing comfortable shoes. It waits. No guilt. No gold star. Just presence. And you—despite all internal protest—eventually reached for it. That's how many of life's better decisions unfold: not with trumpets, but with a shrug and a half-interested glance.

You asked about mindfulness. Mine begins each morning with something so ordinary it would bore most influencers to tears: breathing. I practise a method called box breathing—four counts in, four held, four out. It's not particularly sexy, but neither is hypertension. A few rounds of this and already my mind steadies and my body sharpens— like a dog that's finally remembered it's house-trained. Calm and energy, you'll find, are not opposites. They're just rarely invited to the same party.

After that, I visit what I call my Bliss List. It's a kind of inner jukebox —moments vivid enough to feel again. I see what I saw. I hear what I heard. I let those memories swell until I'm recharged, not by fantasy, but by the truth of things I've already lived. Then, as the feeling crests, I let one phrase ring out in my mind like a minor threat: 'This day is mine'. Not as a boast, but as a warning to whatever nonsense is waiting in my inbox.

You asked about patience. Good. Nobody else is. Modern aspirations are impatient things—hopped-up on caffeine and demanding results by Thursday. We want transformation to arrive all at once, like a perfectly lit epiphany. But most change works more like weathering than lightning. It rubs away at us slowly, until one day we realise we're somehow different, and vaguely annoyed we can't prove when it happened.

I once attended a concert I didn't want to be at. Everything about it was unpromising—the venue was humid, the company over-enthusi-astic, and the music unfamiliar. But somewhere in the second half, a melody slipped in sideways. Unexpected. Unassuming. One note bent into the next, and suddenly, I was no longer enduring the evening—I was held by it. The music hadn't improved. I had. I'd finally stopped resisting and started receiving. That's what most beauty requires: not expertise, but surrender. Preferably the unglam-orous, unguarded kind.

This is the paradox of living fully. We chase certainty like it owes us something. But it's often in the uncertain, unprepared places that wonder gets a word in. Possibility doesn't announce itself. It loiters. And when we finally step forward—shaky and unscripted—it some-times follows.

I've come to call this openness *amouria*. Not a condition. A stance. It's not just about noticing beauty—it's about letting beauty notice you. When we stand before a painting and give it time—not a glance, but a gaze—we stop consuming and start communing. Light doesn't just fall on the canvas. It comes through it. What was visual becomes visceral. We don't admire the art—we're *with* it. And yes, you can do this with coffee too.

To live this way is to choose depth over speed, presence over perfor-mance. It means you won't always be first, but you'll be fully there. And the unexpected reward? When you live in *amouria*, you glow a little. Not for display. But because your joy no longer stops at your skin. It travels—in the way you speak, the way you pause, the care you extend. Even your email tone changes. People will notice. They may not compliment you on it, but they'll quietly gravitate to you.

So let me encourage you, as you go on: keep deepening your experiences. Taste your coffee—don't just survive it. Let the music move you—not just distract you. Think not only of what you're doing, but how it's making you feel. And crucially, return to those moments—remember them, savour them, re-run them like a favourite joke. Joy, like guilt, has a remarkable memory. Use it.

Living this way won't give you perfect days. But it will give you real ones. The kind you can actually feel yourself inside. It's not about being right, or productive, or worthy. It's about showing up—not as a thinker or a fixer, but as a participant. And when enough people do that—when enough people glow quietly—the world tilts, just a little.

This isn't utopia. It's just presence with the volume turned up.

Write soon,

P.

SEVEN
SCROLLING , STILLNESS & SHOWING UP

DEAR P,

I often catch myself halfway through a scroll, forgetting what I was even looking for. It usually happens on a lazy Saturday afternoon, when I tell myself I'm just going to "quickly check" a message. *Just one.* Famous last words. One minute I'm opening Messenger to reply to a friend, and the next thing I know, I'm jumping on different tabs I didn't mean to open. And before I know it, I'm knee-deep in someone else's vacation photos, reels of silly dogs, and updating my grocery list.

My original purpose? Gone. *Poof!* Lost somewhere between reels and endless notes. It's like my brain goes on a joyride the moment I touch my phone. Apps open. Thoughts scatter. I'm left feeling weirdly full and empty at the same time. It's like I consumed a whole bag of mental junk food and I don't even remember tasting it.

It's not just in my phone though. Sometimes I'd walk into my room, determined to get things done and two hours later I'm reorganising my closet and seeing clothes I didn't know I have. I call these my *acci-*

dental productivity. I didn't intend to fold clothes and later on pick up the vacuum, but hey – at least I've done something, right?

All of this to say: sometimes, staying present is hard. I'd like to think that the world is designed to pull us into thousand different directions. And I say this not to shame myself or anyone like me, because for sure I'm not the only one wondering where my attention went or why a quick glance at my phone turned into a 37-minute escape room.

But the good thing about it is that I became aware before it turned into a bad habit. I started noticing the pattern. So instead of beating myself up for getting distracted, I just chose a different reaction towards it. I try to treat it like bumping into an old friend and saying something like, "Oh hey, distraction! Fancy meeting you again, but let's not hangout too long today, okay?"

In that way, I create an escape through laughter and gently return my focus on whatever I was supposed to be doing... like writing this letter. Or drinking my now cold coffee.

And here's the thing I keep learning: being in the moment has to be intentional. It can get messy at times. And when there are moments that I find it hard to go back to what my original plan was, I go back to what you taught me – like the breathing exercises or relaxing my body and to consciously spin the good feeling and quiet the chaos within.

It sounds simple on the outside, but those small practices? They ground me. Whenever I caught myself in the middle of a mental mayhem or feeling overstimulated – I pause to breathe, to really feel the air passing through my nose and coming out my mouth. And just like that, it felt like pressing the reset button.

Other times, I just like to place my hand on my chest or even the top of my head. I make sure to really feel the warmth or the weight of my hand to remind me to calm down and stay in the present. They serve as my physical anchors to reel me back in to reality. There's something grounding about touch – especially my own. It's like telling myself, "You can relax now. It's okay."

Another simple thing that I do is just closing my eyes for a few seconds. I tune in to the sensation of my feet on the floor, the sounds around me, the rhythm of my breath and suddenly the world feels a little less chaotic.

It's in these little things that I find my way back to the present. Not with the big actions or fixed sets of routines but with just simple cues that remind me to come home to myself.

With that, I also wanted to thank you. You've taught me that mindfulness isn't something to be perfected, but something to be practiced. I'm grateful for every piece of wisdom you've shared along the way.

With appreciation,

FG

MY YOUNG FRIEND,

Your letter left me grinning in sympathy. The great victories of the modern age, it turns out, include replying to a message without opening seventeen unrelated tabs or accidentally researching *amphibian policy* in northern Europe. I am aware that Socrates asked questions that shaped Western civilisation. I am also aware that I once Googled 'why are frogs illegal in Norway?' Let's call that a draw!

What I admire about your letter—aside from the charm and quiet insight—is your refusal to moralise the mess. You're not flogging yourself for distraction, nor are you sanctifying presence like a TED Talk in a candlelit yoga barn. You're doing something braver: noticing the pattern, smiling at it, and returning with grace rather than guilt. That, I'd argue, is the beginning of mastery. Yes, you wandered. And then you wandered home.

And what left me wondering is the way you've begun regarding your own attention. You describe it like it's an occasionally mischievous dog: mostly loveable, prone to vanishing and best guided back, not by shouting, but with a *Scooby-Snack* and good timing. I've known monks who could've learned something from that!

I call such scrolling 'research'— only to avoid calling it what it is: *procrastination in lycra*. There's always a *reason* to check one more thing. To follow one more link. To dive deep into the shallow end. And, even if what you find has the sheen of insight, it often leaves the soul faintly malnourished. It seems *binge-learning* is the only mental feast that leaves you intellectually starved.

Still, what matters isn't how often we drift. It's how we respond when we notice the drift. And you've developed something both humorous and heroic: a ritual of return. A breath. A touch. A glance around the room. These aren't just cute coping mechanisms—they're acts of quiet resistance. In an age where progress gave us apps but stole our attention, your hand on your chest is an act of 'rebellion in pyjamas'. I loved it.

You're learning the hard truth: *mindfulness feels nice, until life forgets to behave.* Because being in the moment these days is like rehearsing a sonnet in a riot—romantic in theory, absurd in practice. And riots, as you've noticed, come in many forms: deadlines, headlines, and group chats that could have been emails. So, we adapt. We learn that we can build *stillness* from spare parts: breath, touch, small cues. Some days, my sense of peace is stitched together from a thousand dopey quirks and one perfectly dazed grin.

Your hand on your head, your breath in your body, your eyes closed for three seconds too long—these things matter. They sound absurd.

They *are* absurd. But so is the alternative: handing your mind over to the next reel, the next scroll, the next crisis delivered via glowing rectangle. If the ancients found calm through connection to land, family, and ritual, modern life offers a digital substitute for ancestral rhythm—ritual without roots. So, we plant our own.

You mention how presence, when it arrives, feels like pressing a reset button. Yes. But it's also a performance, isn't it? Equanimity is often a performance of balance—not its achievement. To be calm is to be structured—with the daily burden of pretending it's effortless. I sometimes think mindfulness is not freedom—it's discipline in disguise. But then again, so is love. As is learning. As is any worthwhile human thing.

Let me offer a scene, since you were kind enough to share yours. I was meant to be writing. I had coffee. I had time. I even cleared the table, which in my world passes for ceremonial preparation. Instead, I found myself not writing, but resetting a forgotten password and then falling down a rabbit hole about how multi-tasking might be frying our dopamine receptors. It wasn't work. It wasn't rest. It was loitering in digital limbo—scrolling with the hollow precision of a man determined to avoid confronting his own unfinished paragraph. And all I could think was: *intention is the line between learning and loitering.*

So, I shut the screen. Touched the table. Let the silence spread. Only a few moments, but long enough to return. Living in the moment is admirable—once you've sacrificed the rest of your life preparing for it. This moment is all there is—and I practised for hours to say that casually.

Presence, it seems, isn't where we start. It's where we return to. Again and again, like a stubborn bird finding its way back to a crooked nest. And every return, however clumsy, is a small triumph. The art of presence is the tragedy of needing to learn what was once instinct.

And still—you're learning. Gloriously. Funnily. Honestly. You're making piles out of chaos. Those small practices that ground me? Mostly putting things in slightly nicer piles. Scaffolding doesn't always look noble. Sometimes it's just better stacking.

So, when you next find yourself drifting—your brain mid-scroll, your coffee gone cold, your attention chasing its tail—don't panic. Don't sermonise. Just return. Touch something solid. Breathe. Let yourself laugh at the absurdity of it all. Then decide, quietly, what now?

No script. Just this:

A strong 'drive for completion' is just O.C.D. with better P.R.!

And presence isn't magic—it manifests.

And you, my friend, are learning to maintain with good humour and a warm heart.

Write again when the scroll wins. Or when it doesn't. I'll be here.

P.

EIGHT
THE FLOW STATE PUZZLE

DEAR P,

I've found myself thinking lately about what it means to *get in the zone*. The kind where work feels effortless, time seems to freeze, and I become so absorbed in doing things that everything else fades into the background. You know, the one you call the 'flow state' and others call as 'being locked in'.

But here's the thing, sometimes it doesn't come easily when I ask for it. I can sit at my desk, set the perfect playlist, sip my coffee just the way I like it, open my notes then... *nothing*! Focus scatters. My brain seems to forget what I originally planned to do. And yet, on some days, I might blink and realise that I've been in the zone for two hours without really noticing it. Why is that? Why is it so slippery? I wonder.

Perhaps you've felt the same way. If you've had those moments where everything clicks – and then spent the next moment wondering how to get back. I've read somewhere that some people also experience this. It's like chasing a butterfly – the more you reach for it, the more it flutters away.

I can still remember working on a blog last month. I had been circling the topic for hours, writing a sentence, deleting two, rearranging outlines that felt more like puzzles. I told myself I'd just sit with it for thirty minutes, no expectations, just to move the needle. And then something strange happened. A sentence landed just right. Then another. And another.

I looked up and realised that I've been writing for more than an hour straight – fully in it, no phones, no distractions, although a lot of editing. Well, I guess that's part of it. But I did it. Just pure presence. It felt like I have slipped into some invisible current that led me into flow state.

I've been paying closer attention to what makes that state of flow easier to access. Sometimes it's the environment – a quieter space, fewer tabs open, even the time of day. Other times, it seems to only happen when I stopped trying to 'produce' and just start small then go with it. There's something about easing into the process, rather than expecting or even forcing flow to appear on command, that seems to invite it more naturally.

Perhaps flow doesn't always begin with inspiration or something grand to get you moving. Sometimes, it shows up after I've worked through a bit of resistance or distraction. It's almost like focus doesn't come all at once. It builds up naturally, once I've settled in.

And when it does, it's deeply satisfying, like being fully present and in sync with the task in front of me.

I'm sharing this because I'm genuinely curious if there's a faster and smoother way to be in it. If this is just a matter of experience, or rhythm, or mindset – or a mix of all three? Truth be told, I still stumble at times.

Mental clarity without burnout. Easier said than done, isn't it? What's been working for you? Do you have a pattern or better practices that help you focus and stay in the flow longer without burning the mental gears.

Always curious,

FG

My Young Friend,

You've named it. The ache. The one that haunts artists, writers, athletes—and anyone else who's tried to do something worthwhile on a Monday afternoon with too many tabs open and a brain that behaves like a balloon in a wind tunnel.

You were ready—fully, gloriously ready. The coffee was a symphony. The playlist, liquid motivation. The desk... well, it was clean enough to impress a Scandinavian monk. And yet—nothing.

Focus flickers. Your intentions collapse like a flan in a cupboard. The butterfly buggers off.

You called flow 'slippery'. That's generous. Flow is evasive, temperamental, and pathologically averse to being summoned. It's the emotional equivalent of a cat on a hot tin roof—mystical, beautiful, and deeply uninterested in your plans. But let me offer a different theory.

Flow isn't missing. You're mis-tuned. You see, the Earth orbits in what physicists call the Goldilocks Zone. Not too hot, not too cold. Just right for life to bloom. Drift closer to the sun, we fry. Further out, we freeze. We are—cosmically speaking—here on sufferance and good luck.

Now take that idea and scale it down. To the body. To the breath. To the strange, magnificent orchestra that is your nervous system.

Flow doesn't live in extremes. It thrives in balance. You don't enter it by kicking the door in. You slip into it the way you slip into a warm bath or a good conversation—almost by accident, always by alignment. And alignment isn't a mindset. It's a memory.

A state your body already knows how to reach—if you stop trying to impress it. You asked if there's a faster way. There is. But no one can sell it. Because 'tune your inner jazz trio' doesn't print well on a water bottle. Let me explain.

You've already tasted flow—writing that blog, word by word, sentence by stubborn sentence, until something clicked and time vanished. You softened enough to be moved. You steadied enough to stay upright. That wasn't luck. That was tuning.

Flow is jazz, not accounting. It doesn't follow instructions. It improvises—but only on familiar scales. It doesn't want your anxiety. It wants your readiness. This is not about inspiration. It's about physiology.

Too calm and you nap. Too charged and you combust. But in that breath-held space—between inhale and exhale—where you're neither braced nor bored, neither collapsed nor clenched? That's the entry point.

Flow doesn't shout. It purrs. And if you're listening, it sounds like it's been waiting for you all along. Here's what I believe, after too many failed starts and a few glorious stretches of real-time magic:

Flow comes when three parts of you hum in unison—the animal, the lover, and the librarian. The gut. The heart. The head. All tuned. All alert. All safe. This isn't a contradiction. It's a trinity.

Each must be soothed enough to settle, and thrilled enough to try. So. You want a way in? Not a hack. Not a twelve-step productivity cult. A way back. Then follow me. No urgency. No enlightenment. Just this:

Smell the sea breeze. Not metaphorically. Actually.

Call it back. Salt and ozone. Summer on the edge of your skin. That first inhale where the ocean air hits differently— bright, ancient, oddly electric. As if the Earth is breathing with you.

Feel it now. The breeze brushing your face. Not a gust. A stroke. Over your cheeks. Around your ears. Down your arms. Across your torso. Cool, not cold. Alive. Balanced.

Beneath you—sand. Warm, soft, shifting. It gives way, just slightly. Not enough to lose you. Just enough to remind you: you're real. Each grain, a continent. Let the weight of that wonder settle into your bones.

Now listen. Waves. Crash. Withdraw. Crash. Withdraw. Steady percussion. The metronome of breath. Yours. And not yours.

Taste the air. Bite into citrus. Not polite orange segments. The real deal. Ripe. Tangy. Sun-warmed. Lip-soft. Slightly rude.

That first burst on your tongue—sharp and sweet. Mouth floods. Salivation. Salvation. A small hallelujah. A grin begins to tingle on your skin, all by itself.

Scent follows. Zest and blossom. Almost floral. Almost fire.

And something inside you, begins to open. Your shoulders drop. Your stomach releases. Your legs remember they belong to you.

You are not bracing. You are not escaping. You are here. Fully.

And now—permission. To arouse. To quicken. To write. To create without straining. To move without clenching. To begin. The body says:

'...*now*...'

And just when you think it couldn't get more absurd—you catch someone's eyes. Not beautiful because of symmetry. Beautiful because they've been watching you. All this time. Not judging. Just seeing. And suddenly, you are seen. And within that reflection, a pulse of connection runs across your skin.

Then, a laugh. A child's laugh. Sharp, free, ridiculous. The kind that makes you laugh too, because it reminds you that you still can. Your face softens. Your mouth opens. The breath moves like it knows the way.

And now a smile—one you know. Not a grin. A welcome. Like a door opening across someone's face. Their arms around you. Soft. Sure. As if belonging was never a question.

And above—stars. Silent. Distant. Endless. Your breath matches theirs. You don't have a wish. You have a willingness. Let the dream come. Let the flight begin. Because this—this right here—this symphony of scent and skin and soul? This is the prelude to flow.

This is how we remember who we are. Not with fireworks. But with tuning forks and citrus and salt air. Somewhere between tension and grace—we touch the divine. And like Zhuangzi's butterfly, when we do, we may not know whether we are dreaming or being dreamed. Either way—it will feel just right.

Write again when you're flying. Or stalled and swearing at the air. I'll be here. Tuning.

And listening.

P

NINE
LESSONS LEARNT THE HARD WAY

DEAR P,

There are some lessons in life that arrive gently like soft waves on the shore. Others crash into us like a tidal wave, leaving us gasping for air and unsure which way is up. This is the story about the latter – when everything familiar seemed to fall apart.

Right before the pandemic changed the world, I made the bold and scary decision to resign from my job. I didn't know then that I was walking straight into one of the most uncertain chapters of my life. With no steady income, no clear direction, and the sudden halt of the world as we knew it, I found myself in the middle of a storm I couldn't have predicted. Alongside global crisis, I was also faced with a personal one. Quarter life crisis crept which made me ask questions about who I was and what I was meant to be doing.

To make it even harder, I was far away from my family and friends. Isolation wasn't just a physical state, it became an emotional one for me too. Days blurred into nights and for a while I felt like I was floating in limbo. I was disconnected from the life I had known and the future I had hoped and imagined. It was messy. It was so confusing.

What I didn't know then was that life was teaching me the kind of lessons that can't be rushed – lessons that only reveal themselves when everything else is stripped away.

When I decided to leave my job, I thought I had a good backup plan and that I was choosing uncertainty on my own terms. I believed that with enough planning and courage, I could figure out what came next. But then the big shift happened. The pandemic didn't just interrupt the routines or disrupt plans, it suspended them completely. Suddenly, no one had answers. Jobs disappeared, cities shut down, and the entire world seemed to hold its breath. Any plans I had began to feel irrelevant in a world that no longer followed the rules I once understood.

My personal decision turned into something much bigger, it became a shared global experience of fear of the unknown. But even with that shared uncertainty, I felt alone. The silence and stillness outside mirrored a confusion deep within me. I was in my mid-twenties, resigned from a stable job, far from home and unsure of who I was without my usual roles and responsibilities. The quarter life crisis hit hard, and there was nowhere to hide from it.

Without distractions, I had to sit with myself – and it wasn't always pretty. Doubts, negative self-talk and disconnection crept in. Questions I had long avoided surfaced: *What do I really want? How will I survive this? What really is my purpose for being here?* These thoughts were loud. The weight of adulting expectations and overwhelming pressure broke me.

It was uncomfortable in ways I can't fully explain. There were days when I felt completely lost. I grieved for the parts of me that I had outgrown and those missed moments I had that won't happen again. The lack of clarity wasn't only frustrating, it was paralysing.

Then in one disturbingly quiet morning and probably with the lack of good sleep, I found myself writing on my journal, *"Maybe the point isn't to figure it all out. Maybe it is to sit with the unknown."* And that stopped me.

For the first time in months, I began to see that the more I resisted discomfort, the heavier it became. But when I accepted it for what it is, it felt a little bit lighter. There was still some worry of course, but at that time I began to let it go and just let it happen without stressing about it too much. That's when it clicked, that pain and discomfort was trying to teach me something.

I started reconnecting with things that once made me feel alive – reading for joy, writing without force, and catching up with friends without feeling drained. Once I stopped worrying about the unknown, I began to feel grounded. I wasn't "back on track" in the traditional sense, but I was starting to build something much more meaningful. It's a life that didn't depend on strict routines and plans to feel worthwhile.

I allowed myself to be a beginner again, to explore different paths that I hadn't considered before. I trusted that even small steps were steps forward. I also started opening up more – to the people I trusted, to the opportunities I once dismissed, and most importantly to myself. I learned that I didn't have to have everything figured out to be enough. That season of pause became less about waiting and more about becoming.

And that's when it truly hit me – the hard way had been the only way for me to *really* listen. Not just to the world, but to my own voice which was buried under years of expectations, noise and busyness. What I thought was the end of something for me turned out to be the beginning of a more honest version of myself.

Now, I can look back on that season and see that it was a deep recalibration. It tested my faith, my sanity and my whole sense of purpose.

It wasn't easy and I wouldn't wish that kind of loneliness and disorientation on anyone, but I also wouldn't trade what it taught me. The discomfort was brutal, yes, but it did its work.

If I could talk to the version of me back then who's curled up in uncertainty, feeling lost and behind, I'd say: "You're not drowning, you're learning how to swim." And if I could tell anyone who's going through a similar experience, I'd tell them to trust the tide. Even the roughest waves eventually bring us to the shore. A little drained but definitely stronger and far more ourselves than when we first set out.

How about you, dear friend, where are the waves carrying you lately?

All the best,

FG

Dear FG,

Some events don't begin with a bang but with a cancellation. You wake up and the life you were meant to be living has closed for renovations. Indefinitely. No warning, no refund. Possibly replaced by a less attractive substitute—think: you ordered 'purpose and clarity' but received 'existential soup with a side dish of bills'.

That's how your letter read. Not like a story, but like weather—rolling in fast, unapologetic. You thought you were making a brave choice, stepping out of one job into possibility. And then, right on cue, the world decided to fold in on itself. Not a poetic storm. A bureaucratic apocalypse. Borders closed. Plans suspended. Momentum lost.

It's a very human tale. Older than cities, older than language. We make maps. The world remakes itself. We try to follow old roads across a new landscape and find ourselves circling back to nowhere.

I've lived through a few of those metamorphoses. My marriage ended after sixteen years. That kind of loss doesn't announce itself—it accumulates, like dust behind furniture you stopped moving. I lived, loved, and remarried, thankfully.

But not before being drenched in emotional weather best described as bleak, with unexpected showers of bitterness and the occasional sharp hail of self-recrimination. Because, if one bubble is burst, it may be regarded as a tragedy. For them all to burst together begins to resemble a need for a map upgrade.

And grief, well. Grief doesn't even pretend to care for narrative arc. My father, my brother, and my son all died young. Each one carved a separate hollow. Each demanded a different kind of breathing just to make it through the day. And yet I'm still here. Somehow. Bent, not broken. Which sounds poetic but feels more like waking up on a stranger's couch with someone else's headache.

Then there was the restaurant. My livelihood, my tempo, my open wound of a dream. Gone. Just... gone. A casualty of economics, timing, and, if I'm honest, ego. I could have wallowed—and I did—I indulged for a fortnight. There may have been whisky. There was certainly toast. Grief wears many outfits. Mine wore a singlet and shorts and delivered monologues to two wee confused dogs.

You describe that moment of total confusion—the paralysis, the silence, the ache of not knowing who you are anymore. I call that being naked in the rain. It's visceral, isn't it? No shelter, no script, no skin thick enough to hold out the cold. You're just there. Soaked. Hoping the storm gets bored and moves on. It rarely does.

You feel like the lead in your own hero's journey—but instead of being cast as The Rock, it turns out you're Jack Black, screaming through a game of Jumanji you didn't sign up for.

But something else happens too. When the wind stops screaming and the air goes still, you realise you're still breathing. Not well. Not easily. But enough. And then, like you did, you start scribbling truths into notebooks. 'Maybe the point isn't to figure it all out.' That line, by the way, deserves a plaque. Or a tea towel. Maybe both. Because most of us are out here trying to spreadsheet the meaning of life while it's clearly being written in crayon.

That wasn't giving up. That was adaptation. Which is the real super-power. Not bouncing back but bending in the right places. Redrawing your map mid-stride because the old one no longer fits the terrain.

This is the job of neuro-resilience. We're not here to suffer nobly. We're here to recover quickly. To shrink the time between impact and integration. To shorten our stay in the cocoon—and to lessen the need to ever go back in. We do this by learning how to update our mental maps in real time, to let the world wobble without assuming we're broken. To let the body settle again into a state that says: you're safe enough to move.

And here's the dangerous secret: the deepest healing doesn't happen in pain. It happens in joy. In pleasure. In moments of connection that let us remember who we were before the roles and expectations closed in. When you started reading again, writing without pressure, calling friends without dreading the call that wasn't a return to normal. That was the beginning of becoming.

The trouble with transformation is that it never consults your calendar. It arrives uninvited, drinks all your wine, and asks difficult questions about your childhood. But once you stop trying to tidy it away, it starts making sense—like modern art or bad karaoke: painful, revealing, and somehow... essential.

You didn't find your old self. You found something new. Still fragile. Still forming. But more honest. And if I could bottle that process and hand it to every young person who thinks they're lost when they're really just growing—like scruffy puppies shedding the wrong fur—I would in a heartbeat.

But the best I can do is this: tell you that what you lived through has been lived through before. And yet it is yours, singular and irreplaceable. The tide that swallowed you also taught you how to breathe differently.

Now comes the second half of the journey: not just emerging, but teaching. Helping others navigate their cocoon with less shame, more speed. Fewer detours through despair. Because the butterfly must always emerge. That's not optimism. That's biology. The cocoon is not a dwelling. It's a workshop. A temporary space for transformation. Not a place to live in—just a place to pass through.

So yes, you made it. You didn't drown. You learned how to swim. Badly, at first. Like a startled toddler thrown into the deep end of an Olympic pool. But swim you did—and not in circles. Inward. Then forward.

As for me, you asked where the waves are carrying me lately. Truth is, I've stopped trying to predict the tide. These days, I let the current have its way—so long as I can still laugh, still write, still hold those I love with both hands. I don't need the map to be perfect. I just need it to move with me.

We'll meet again, you and I. Somewhere between chaos and calm. Wings still damp. Flying anyway.

And if not flying, at least gliding with panicked elegance.

Yours,

P

TEN
BRIGHT-EYED, READY AND... CLUELESS

DEAR P,

When I was just starting out as a young professional, there's this kind of excitement that I couldn't quite contain. I stepped into a new world with a head full of ideas, a heart full of ambition and a strong belief that I'm going to do things differently. I had this drive to not just clock in and out, that I was there to contribute, to innovate and make my mark. And for a while that drive carried me.

In the beginning, everything felt possible. I read books, absorbed advice from different mentors, observe seniors and told myself that I was ready. I dressed the part, adopt the jargon, rehearse over and over. I even convinced myself – even though I was new and maybe a little uncertain, that by showing up with enough energy and purpose, the world would meet me halfway. I had the enthusiasm of someone who hadn't yet been told "that's not how we do things here."

But slowly, reality started to show itself. That's where I started to notice that even with all the right energy, systems rarely bend for the new ones. So quickly I adapted. I picked my battles. I started to mimic what works, even if it didn't feel quite like me.

They don't really tell you that sometimes, faking it feels easier than fighting it. That in the middle of all your big dreams, you'll find yourself quietly shrinking – nodding in rooms where you want to ask questions, saying yes when your gut says no. You think it's just temporary. Just a phase. Just until you've "made it."

But over time, the act gets heavy. I began to wonder if maybe I was losing parts of myself in exchange for acceptance and what's easy. I wonder if the younger version of myself, the one who was optimistic to get started, would even recognise me.

And that's where the saying crept in – *"Fake it til you make it."*

At first, it sounded harmless. Even empowering. It's like a code passed around to remind us that we don't need to have it all figured out, we just need to *look* like we do. Wear confidence like a second skin. Nod, smile, deliver. Quiet the questions and doubts. Edit the emotions. Package yourself as someone who's okay with everything.

But somewhere along the way, it stopped being a peptalk and started becoming a survival tactic. I faked composure when I was overwhelmed. Faked agreement when I was silently disagreeing. Faked enthusiasm in meetings where my ideas are either immediately dismissed or loudly trashed. The line between learning and performing began to blur, until I was no longer sure whether I was growing or just getting better playing the part.

There were days I felt like a ghost version of myself – present, polished, performing, but always slightly out of alignment with who I really was. I remember nodding in meetings, jotting down notes I didn't believe in, putting effort into things that felt hollow. And it wasn't because I didn't care. It was because I cared *so much* that I thought this was what I had to do to survive.

The truth is, systems are built to reward sameness. Stability. Predictability. So when you enter the workforce with boldness, vision and hunger to shake things up, it's not always welcomed. And when resistance gets you nowhere, it becomes easier to just *blend in.* To stop offering a different voice, because different always feels like a risk.

Over time, I slowly felt the burnout. I started to doubt my own instincts. I questioned whether I was ever cut out for the job. I wondered if maybe the ones who just go with the flow had it right all along.

But here's something I wish I learned earlier: You don't have to fake it. Not forever. Not even now. All I had to do was to be honest, to align with what I truly felt. And I cannot do all those without feeling safe from the skin in. I had to drop my guard down in order to see that I can be completely safe without pretending. All I needed was a nudge from you.

It wasn't easy. But the moment I stopped performing and started *being*, something inside me softened. I no longer constantly calculate my next move or brace for impact. I started to listen more and be more present. And slowly, I began to see that the rooms I once entered with tension began to feel different, not because they changed, but because *I* did.

And that's why I'm writing you this letter – to thank you for that nudge. You reminded me of something I nearly forgot: that I never needed to be anything other than who I am becoming. You didn't need me to have it all figured out. You simply asked me to be present, to slow down and breathe.

I learned that the pressure to "make it" often makes us overlook that progress we're already making. That my best 10 today will always be different, and often better than my 10 yesterday. Each day brings a new version of what my best can be. That confidence doesn't come from knowing everything, it comes from trusting that I'll find my own way even if I stumble. That the rooms where I feel safe to speak my truth are the ones worth staying in. And that it's okay to outgrow the roles I once felt I had to play.

I also learned that alignment matters. That the body knows when we're out of sync with our values, even when the performance looks better. That no amount of external validation can replace the peace that comes from internal honesty. Sometimes, all we need is a whisper of, "You can drop your shoulders now, you're safe."

So thank you – not just for reminding me but for holding the mirror. For asking the questions that didn't need answers, only honesty. It helped me a lot to come back to myself with a little more softness and a lot more truth.

I don't know exactly what tomorrow will ask of me, but I do know this: I won't trade authenticity for approval again. And if I ever find myself tempted to shrink or fake it again, I'll remember this: I'm allowed to grow out of it. That my voice, my pace, my new 10 today – it's enough. It always was.

With grace and gratitude,

FG

Dear FG,

There's a moment in every performance when the actor forgets they're acting. The lights blur. The applause fades. The smile stiffens. And suddenly, you're no longer playing the role—you've become it. Trapped inside a version of yourself built for someone else's expectations. That was the part of your letter that stayed with me. Not just the bright-eyed beginning—that was brave. But the quiet recognition that somewhere between the enthusiasm and the eye-rolls, the part of you that once said,

"Not me. I'll do this differently"

...had gone quiet. Respectfully silent. Waiting for permission that never came. I've known that silence.

You hear it in the way your voice lifts when speaking to those in power. In the way your shoulders rise before meetings and don't drop until bedtime. It's the silence of someone whose nervous system has negotiated a deal it never agreed to: compliance in exchange for shelter. You wrote:

"I wonder if the younger version of myself would even recognise me."

And I felt that like a bruise. Because the truth is, she probably would —and she'd ask why you were looking so tired. But you were not broken. You were adjusting. Because the role you were asked to play was never meant for someone fully alive. The system wasn't built for boldness—it was built for repetition. And when your presence threatened to change its rhythm, it responded with resistance: boldness would be encouraged—as long as it's wearing beige and agrees to take minutes.

So, you adapted. You mimicked. Smiled. Nodded. Took notes on things you didn't believe. Not out of weakness, but survival. Because the rooms you were in rewarded quiet. And presence. And sameness. But performance is expensive. Not in effort—in presence.

By that point, your main transferable skill was pretending to care in three time zones.

Yes, they call it *"Fake it till you make it"*. As if confidence were a costume you wear long enough to become real. But your body knows better. Faking calm. Faking agreement. Faking enthusiasm when what you really feel is anything but—that's not poise. That's a poker face cracking under pressure. The kind your nervous system was never meant to sustain. It's not a character flaw. It's a physiological conflict.

You might not hear it at first. But it shows up eventually. In the mirror. In the stillness before sleep. In that quiet moment when you think:

"This isn't who I meant to be."

That's the real cost of faking it. Because pretending doesn't build capacity—it burns it. You spend energy maintaining a version of yourself you don't believe in. And the body keeps the score in fatigue, fractured sleep, and the low-grade dread that builds around Monday. This isn't about fragility. It's about fidelity. Not to the system. To yourself. Because confidence was never meant to be performed. It was meant to be felt.

Now, let's talk about that—*confidence*—not the TEDx kind, not the arms-akimbo soundbite. The grounded kind. The kind that doesn't raise its voice or ask for permission. Confidence isn't volume. It's congruence. The jaw softens. The breath evens. The tongue unglues from the roof of the mouth. And there it is—not a transformation, but a return.

Confidence doesn't arrive with fireworks. It lands quietly. Familiar. Yours.

That's why faking it is so costly. Because your body already knows how to generate the real thing—if you stop interrupting it with performance. You don't need to fake feeling good. You can create good feel-ing. Not with slogans or borrowed mantras, but with sensation. With memory. With the quiet art of restoring safety and letting confidence emerge from that ground. And no, that doesn't mean buying a grati-tude journal and pretending it wasn't a rebranded to-do list.

Because joy, as it turns out, isn't a side-effect. It's a signal. And you can build it. So, let's retire the phrase: *"fake it till you make it"* has done its damage. It's had its time. It promised a shortcut. What it delivered was burnout. With a smile. So, here's something better:

• *Feel it now... and remember forever.*

Because that's what you're doing now—you're remembering some-thing that you had forgotten how to do. Showing up without three layers of translation between your gut and your words. You said it best:

"I don't need to fake it anymore."

You never did. You didn't need fixing. You needed safety. And now that safety lives inside you. That younger version of you—the one with the fire and the plan—she wasn't naïve. She was whole—and waiting for you to remember. What followed wasn't disillusionment. It was erosion. Tiny edits to your voice until it barely sounded like you. But you didn't lose her. You gave her something: discernment.

You didn't outgrow her. You outlived the belief that you had to shrink in order to belong. And that's not surrender. That's evolution. Align-ment isn't a luxury. It's leverage. The difference between walking into a room braced for impact... or entering like your spine belongs there.

When your inner state matches your outer stance, there's no transla-tion tax. No conversion cost. Your system exhales. And you speak without effort. Not because you've been trained—but because you're finally congruent. And now that you're no longer translating yourself to be tolerated, your signal gets cleaner. Stronger. Sharper. Not louder—truer. The rooms that once required performance will feel different—not because they changed, but because now you enter aligned. You don't scan for permission. You set tone. And when you do, others will feel it. Because alignment isn't just efficient—it's contagious. That's not "soft skills". That's structural efficiency. And it's just beginning.

You wrote:

"Sometimes, all we need is a whisper of, 'You can drop your shoulders now, you're safe.'"

So here it is. Louder now: *just drop them.* You're safe. You were always safe. It's just that no one told your jaw. You've stopped bartering authenticity for approval. That's the quiet revolution. The kind that doesn't announce itself with a mic drop—just the steady refusal to shrink in rooms that punish truth. You've remembered something essential: *that calm isn't earned—it's allowed.*

And that the right spaces don't require a costume. They just require you. And now, when you walk into those rooms, your younger self will still recognise you. Possibly roll her eyes, shake her head, and *tut.* But she'll stay in the room. Not because you stayed the same. But because you remembered who you were always becoming.

In time, you'll catch yourself in moments of unguarded clarity—saying the thing no one else will, and watching the room soften. Not because you raised your voice, but because your voice came from somewhere real. That's not rebellion. That's leadership.

Write again soon.

P

INTERLUDE—WHAT THE THRESHOLD ASKS

There are rooms you no longer fit in. And not because they shrank.

You stopped contorting. You stopped interpreting silence as safety, and speed as competence.

You are no longer the teacher who needs to know everything.

Just the one who remembers what it means to listen.

And so here you are—on the lip of another room.

The old voice says:

"Earn your entry".

The new voice asks:

"Are you still willing to bring your whole self in?"

If you must knock, let it be on your own ribcage.

Then step through.

Let love meet you not as performance, but as presence.

ELEVEN

LOVE IS A VERB, NOT A NOUN

DEAR P,

We grow up thinking that love is something we find. We chase it in people, in moments, in movies that promise happy endings. It's easy to believe love is a feeling, something that sweeps in, takes over, and stays if it's "meant to be." But life, with its slow mornings, hard days and extraordinary choices, taught me something different: love is not something you fall into. Love is something you *do*.

This truth didn't come in one big realisation. It was shaped unhurriedly. It was shaped by being raised by a single mother who never said "I love you" out loud, not because she didn't feel it, but because she believed showing up was *saying it*. That, I've come to realise was her love in action. Through classrooms where students couldn't always express their feelings, but taught me the language of attention, patience and presence. Through adult relationships where promises came easy but effort was scarce.

For most of my life, I mistook love for a noun. An idea. A destination. But real love, meaningful and genuine, doesn't sit still waiting to be felt. It shows up. It acts. And it looks different in every stage of life. This is a reflection of those stages: from the silent love of a mother, to the chaos of teaching, to the relationships that tested the meaning of commitment – all of them showing me that love lives in action, not just intention.

Growing up with a single mother, especially in an Asian household, love didn't look like what I saw on TV. There were no heart-to-heart talks or open lighthearted conversations. Instead, there was a different language. A language of ironing our school uniforms late at night, quietly budgeting every cent, and experimenting with what- ever resources we had to create something warm on the table. She never said it out loud, but her every move screamed:

I'm here. I'm trying. I love you.

As a child, I sometimes questioned it. I envied kids with visibly affec- tionate parents, not realising that love isn't always loud. It took years, and becoming an adult myself, to realise that love, for her, was survival and sacrifice. It was showing up, no matter how tired she was. Her love didn't live in words. It lives in what she does, day in and out, without expecting anything in return.

As I stepped into adulthood, I found myself in another unexpected place where love – this time, in its most patient and persistent form – was constantly being called out of me: *the classroom.*

I remember one particular lesson we had – teaching the parts of speech. We identified nouns, adjectives, verbs. When we came to "verb", I explained how it's an action word, the part that makes a sentence come alive. At that time, I never thought much beyond the textbook definition. But now, looking back, I find myself returning to that lesson in a new way. It's because love, I realise, is a verb, an action word. It's what we *do* every day – in small moments and big ones.

I didn't expect teaching to teach me so much about love. But it did – because to teach well, you must first *care*. You must choose love every single day, even when patience wore thin, your energy drained, and efforts go unnoticed. And just like love, teaching doesn't look the same for every teenager.

With them, love takes on a more complex shape. It's giving them room to wrestle with big questions, while offering structure. It's listening without rushing to fix, respecting their silence, and gently calling them back when they drift too far. Some students will challenge everything you say and make you question everything you know. Others will barely meet your eyes or talk. But loving them means showing up anyway.

It means staying consistent, even when they don't. Loving them is choosing not to take things personally when they push you away or when they give hurtful comments. It's listening to their stories no matter how shallow or heart-breaking they are. Waiting for them to gather the courage to speak up and be the first to celebrate their small wins.

I remember being in their position and questioning what I needed back then – what kind of adult could've made a difference for me. I kept turning that question over in my head.

What can I do differently for them?

Sometimes, it's offering a second chance when they expect to be reprimanded. Other times, it's simply noticing them, really noticing, on a day when they feel invisible. It's choosing to respond with curiosity instead of control, patience instead of power. I can't undo what the world has already told them, but I thought that maybe I can be someone who help them unlearn it especially the *not-so-pretty* bits.

Because the truth is, not every student will remember the lessons I've taught – but they will remember how I made them feel. And if I can leave even one of them with the sense that they were seen, heard, and respected, then that's love in action. That's love doing the quiet, steady work of believing in someone before they know how to believe in themselves.

And maybe that's why I've come to treasure my friendships even more. Because love isn't just a feeling that lives in family or classrooms, it lives in the steady actions of the people who choose to believe and stay. The ones who show up not out of obligation, but choice. I've learned that friendship is a kind of love that moves and acts – sometimes complex but always in motion.

With friends, love looks like remembering hard dates without being reminded. Sending a message just to check in, not because something's wrong but because you genuinely care. It's sitting in silence when words feel too heavy. It's a shared meal, a safe rant, a long pause between replies. Loving friends is an active choice – it doesn't demand attention but gives it freely. And that giving, that showing up, becomes a kind of home.

But as much as friendship has taught me about love, romantic relationships have shown me its complexity in a different light. Because love between partners isn't just presence or care, it's also about trust and sometimes, risk. It's the place where our deepest hopes and fears meet, and where love must stretch and grow – or sometimes, break.

Being in romantic relationship means learning that love isn't always easy or comfortable. It demands even more intentional action. It's not enough to *feel* love, it must be *shown* through consistent choices and actions. It's choosing to communicate honestly, to forgive, to support and to be present not only for the good days but for the hard ones too.

It means choosing to listen rather than reacting impulsively, and working together through conflict instead of walking away. In this way, love isn't static – it's active, alive and ever growing. The verb form of love is what sustains relationships through uncertainty and change. A reminder for us that love is something we do, not just something we say.

So no matter what kind of relationship we build, one thing is clear: love is not a static noun or an abstract idea. Love is action. It's the choices we make, the patience we show, the presence we offer, and the care we give, again and again.

Taylor Swift once sang:

"And you understand now why they lost their minds and fought the wars,

And why I've spent my whole life trying to put it into words,

'Cause you can hear it in the silence,

You can feel it on the way home,

You can see it with the lights out..."

Maybe that's what love really is – a force so powerful it moves beyond words and definition.

How about you, P? What does love *look like* in your life right now? Not the feeling, but the doing. I'm eager to know if you'd be willing to share.

Choosing love in action,

FG

Dear FG,

There's a moment in your last letter—quiet, almost shy—where the page seems to hesitate. It's the kind of line most readers would glide over. But I stopped. Re-read it. Circled it in the mind's margins like a teacher preparing to say:

'Here. This is where it turned.'

You wrote:

'Love isn't something you fall into. Love is something you do.'

There it was. The pivot. Not just an idea worth quoting in chalk across a school corridor, but a shift in weather. The kind of realisation that doesn't just change your mind—it changes the *atmosphere* in your body.

You have bloomed, FG. Not in the *Instagrammable* way. In the way that matters: through tension, survival, and the kind of patience usually reserved for civil servants and saplings. You sprouted a flower from a seed that spent most of its life wondering if the sun had forgotten it.

And yet, as your unofficial gardener, I must say: lovely though it is, this flower is not the end. It is the herald. The signal. The bit before the fruit. There's more, FG. And you're ready for it. You see, before there was the bloom, there was the *ache*. That slow, aching scan for warmth. The bodily hope that someone might say it—just say it—so you wouldn't have to guess.

You weren't being dramatic. You were being *mammal*. But I won't get neuroscientific on you. Let's just say the wiring was working perfectly. You were looking for what every child is told they don't need but absolutely do: the *gesture*, the *tone*, the *signal*. A hug. A wink. A proud nod. A *'bloody well done'*. That's the sort of thing you were hungry for. And you were clever enough to make sense of its absence. To reason with it. To tell yourself:

'Maybe it lives somewhere else. Maybe love isn't a feeling at all. Maybe it's what you do.'

That reframe didn't arrive as a parade. It came disguised as work—early mornings, patient silences, staying after class when your body wanted to leave. You called it duty. And because you're kind, you called it love. You found rhythm. You made reliability the new romance. And something in your body—bless it—finally exhaled. It worked. That's what makes this complicated. You were right. But not *complete.*

Because in crafting love as action, you protected yourself from the sharpest pang: the risk of wanting more. Of admitting that—yes, damn it—you still wanted to be told. Wanted to be held. Wanted not just to be *understood* but *celebrated.* And here's the part we don't write down in lesson plans or staff room mugs: many people stop here. At dutiful love. They build cathedrals from the grind, mistake consistency for intimacy, and call it a day.

But you've written past that. I see the pages turning. You're starting to notice the grey. Reliable love is safe, yes. But it's also steel. Strong. Cold. Unscented. Love that endures but doesn't delight. That's the space you're describing now—the narrow bridge between survival and abundance. You've built something weatherproof. Now comes the question that gives it soul:

> *Can this love—this sturdy, worthy, quietly sacrificial*
> *love—be made lovely?*

The answer, as you might suspect, is yes. But not by working harder. Not by reinforcing the structure. The flower doesn't become fruit by gritting its petals. It softens. It ripens. It opens *again.* That's what this second blooming is. Not a correction of the first. A continuation.

You once believed love was a noun—an object, out there, hoarded or withheld. That belief hurt. It came from the body and was handed over to the brain for repair. The brain did its job. Rebuilt the scaffold. Designed the system. Translated longing into labour. But now, it's time to go the other way. Let the body teach the brain what it knows next.

Because love isn't just what you do when no one notices. Love is an 'as well as'... because it's what you do when someone will notice too. It's the smile you return, not out of politeness but joy. It's the pride you don't swallow, the compliment you say out loud, the hand you hold because the moment called for it. It's the colour returning to the lines. The warmth re-entering the house you built for others.

You've survived the winter. But this next season? This one's for fruit. The thing about steel—strong as it is—is that it doesn't sing. It holds bridges, not birthday cards. It doesn't laugh at your jokes or tear up during school plays. You've built something necessary.

Now comes the part that's *alive*. Reliable love, on its own, is impressive. It deserves a standing ovation. It also gets lonely. There's a moment, after the scaffolding is up and the roof stops leaking, where you realise the house is quiet. Serviceable. Safe. But cold. You've mastered the architecture. Now it's time for décor. And no, I don't mean bunting and scented candles. I mean warmth. I mean the kind of light that doesn't come from a lightbulb.

Because what's missing from your description isn't function. It's colour. Not the pastel kind they sell in aspirational catalogues. I mean the bold, joyful kind that startles you back into remembering you're a person. You've proven you can survive anything. That's not the question anymore. The question now is whether you'll allow yourself to enjoy the thing you've made. Or if you'll keep waiting for permission that doesn't need issuing.

Here's the truth I suspect you already know but were waiting for me to say out loud so you wouldn't feel foolish for wanting it:

You are allowed to want love that is <u>lovely</u>.

Not just earned. Not just endured. But textured, soft, affirming. Love that hugs first and explains later. That compliments your earrings and means it. That uses your name in full sentences like it was chosen deliberately. You're ready for it now. Not because you've been good. But because you've grown. You've earned the right to *soften* without crumbling.

This is the *second punctuation*. And it's not about adding more to your workload. It's about letting beauty in. The same way your students sometimes need reminding they're allowed to smile without a punchline; you too can allow yourself moments of <u>colour without consequence</u>. Not everything you give has to be noble. Not every act of love has to be an unpaid internship in someone else's growth.

Sometimes it's the joke you whisper when no one else is listening. Sometimes it's looking in the mirror and saying, finally:

'I'm proud of me'

It's the moment after the lesson, when a student lingers—not because they're confused, but because for ten seconds, they felt completely safe in your presence. And it's not just about them anymore.

This colour? It's for *you*.

Now that we're here—knees in the soil, flower blooming behind us, sun making its first proper entrance—let's talk fruit.

The fruit of all this, FG, isn't just more students served, more friends held, more days endured without complaint. That's the *yield*. The fruit, though—the real prize—is *the flavour*.

It's the difference between feeding people and *nourishing* them. Between teaching out of obligation and teaching out of affection. Between saying 'You matter' through consistent policy and saying it through a grin that says,

'I actually like you, and it surprises me daily.'

You don't need to change your structure. You need to *saturate* it. Pour yourself into it with colour, rhythm, scent, absurdity. You know— human stuff.

You remember those love languages you once starved for? They're not relics. They're ingredients. Add them in. Not just for others. For you. You've done the dutiful thing. You've ticked all the boxes on the resilience rubric. Now go off-script. Say the thing. Hug first. Add glitter. Call a student 'brilliant' and mean it before the assessment confirms it. Touch a shoulder. Compliment a shirt. Let your face light up like it missed someone, even if they were only gone for a weekend. This isn't indulgence. It's completion.

Let your acts of love feel like love.

That's the fruit. The synthesis. The whole orchestra tuning to the same key. Let's be clear: this isn't about turning your classroom into a greeting card aisle. It's about allowing the *joyful expression of the effort you've already been making*.

You've been holding the weight. Now learn to lift your face. You've been reliable. Now become radiant. And don't be surprised if it startles a few people. That's how they'll know it's real. And that's how you'll know you've stopped performing love and started *living* it. The bud has become a bloom. Now, let it fruit.

And now we come to it—the third bloom. Not a new flower this time, but something quieter. A softening, not a spectacle. You see, the first bloom was survival. The second, structure. But this one—this one is sweetness. The fruit doesn't shout its arrival. It doesn't perform. It ripens. Silently. As if it always knew. That's the stage you're in now. Not yearning. Not proving. Not even enduring. Just *offering*— without losing anything in the giving.

The old models of love taught you to wait, to brace, to earn. Your new one taught you to act, to persist, to remain. This next one will teach you to *glow*. Not in the curated, sun-drenched way of lifestyle influencers or wellbeing posters. I mean the kind of glow that happens when someone looks at you and says, without irony or prompting,

'God, it's good to see you'

And you believe them. Because you've become the kind of person who allows love to be felt—not just confirmed. You've stopped asking for permission to be loved in a way that suits your nervous system. And you've started *giving that kind of love away*—freely, fully, without keeping score. And that's the miracle.

You are beginning to give the acts of love in the lovely way your younger self once craved. You are becoming the very person that child waited for, all those years ago. You're saying the words you longed to hear. You're giving the hug before the apology. You're putting the fruit in other people's hands—*'as well as'* tasting it yourself.

This is not your final form. But it is a damn good one. *Let it be lovely.* Let your structure sparkle. Let your steadiness smile. Let your resilience dance, glittering and on purpose. Let the people around you see that *love doesn't have to be earned,* or endured, or dissected. That it can also be silly. And sincere. Always human.

Let your students see what joy looks like when it comes wrapped in credibility. Let your friends see what kindness looks like when it comes without a catch. Let the people you love hear it—*really hear it*—before they wonder if they're worthy. Because they are. All of them. And so are you. You've done enough surviving, my young friend. Now it's time to *ripen.* Let the third bloom begin.

Yours, fruitfully,

P

PS – You asked what love looks like in my life. Not the feeling. The doing. So here it is.

Love looked like sitting beside my friend, who was suffering horribly from oesophageal cancer. Hypnotising him, guiding him gently back through the corridors of memory—past the pain, past the despair—until we found the boy he used to be. In that softened state, he remembered hiding a toy in the bottom of a wardrobe his father had made for him, a wardrobe that was still upstairs. He went up. Found it. Brought down a small red double-decker London bus.

And then he cried. Not from pain—but from the grief and relief of remembering. My job, in that moment, was to help him giggle through his tears. I asked,

"How long had it been there?"

He said,

"Almost sixty-five years."

I nodded solemnly and said,

"How very disappointing."

He looked at me, puzzled.

I smiled.

"Normally, with London buses, you wait for ages and three come at once!"

He gave me a grin. A proper one. I took it and stretched it into a belly laugh—his first in months. Maybe years. That, FG, is what love looked like that day.

As a big, burly bloke, love also looks like the moments I allow myself to be comforted. When I lost my son. When I lost my enterprise. When I lost my way. Those moments made me raw and touch-sensitive—but healing begins in the good feeling. And touch, real touch, begins the process. I learned that to let people in, you have to open up. And to open your mind to others' ideas, you have to open your heart to their presence.

When I cook for my family, love is in the quiet detail—a thousand little things done with care. The reward? Their clean plates, their satisfied silence. When my dogs go wild with joy, love is lapping up the moment as eagerly as they lap from their bowls. When my wife leaves for work, love is making sure she knows—not thinks, but knows —that she is the most beautiful and sexiest woman alive. And that she feels it in her bones.

When my daughter is scared, love is the knowledge that I would put my body between her and danger. And when she is triumphant, love is the sound of me—whooping, yelling, cheering like a man with no shame and all the joy in the world.

Because love is not a trickle. It's a flood when it's ready. It's presence when it counts. It's laughter through tears and touch without armour.

Because, as the old song goes:

"The greatest thing you'll ever learn

Is just to love and be loved in return."

That's what love looks like for me, FG.

And today, love looks like me writing a letter to a young friend and answering her questions the best way that I can... for her.

P

TWELVE
TAKING THE GARBAGE OUT

DEAR P,

I hope this letter finds you breathing a little more gently today.

I just happened to think about one of our conversations – the one where we joked about how "taking the garbage out" felt oddly therapeutic. Taking the garbage out is something that not all of us look forward to. It's smelly, inconvenient, sometimes even overwhelming – especially when it's been neglected for too long. But it has to be done. Otherwise, it just piles up, rotting in the corners.

You said that our minds work the same way. We collect things we don't need anymore – old wounds, worn-out stories, secondhand shame, we tuck them into our emotional cupboards, telling ourselves we'll deal with them later. And then, just like the garbage, they start to stink.

I used to think myself as a realist, but most days I leaned toward the pessimist side of things. I've often felt safer expecting the worst, assuming the weight of everything, and preparing for disappointment before hope can surprise me. It's not exactly graceful, but it has felt like a form of protection – a way of keeping the chaos at bay.

When life has handed you more than your fair share of sudden storms, you learn to board up the windows even on sunny days. You brace. You prepare. You hold your breath just in case the worst is waiting around the corner. The trouble is, that kind of bracing becomes a habit, and over time, it stiffens everything – your shoulders, your smile, your trust in the present moment. Until you cannot fully enjoy the present without expecting something worse to happen next.

That's the thing about PTSD I guess. It doesn't always show up as screaming or shaking. Sometimes it's just quiet. It narrows your vision. It puts you in a different kind of trance, one where you're not really here. You might be standing in your kitchen, folding laundry, even laughing at something – but part of you is stuck elsewhere, reliving a moment that already ended or fearing one that hasn't even come.

During our sessions of 'taking the garbage out', I've started noticing something else. There's a kind of calm that showed up, like some kind of meditation (although not exactly it). But it's a shift. It's a moment when the usual noise quiets down just enough for something honest to surface. It's an altered state – not the dramatic or mystical way most perceived it to be – that makes the cleaning possible. You see what you've been avoiding and what you've ignored for years. You see what you no longer need.

And that's why I've started to pay attention to the garbage. Not just the trash bin, but the mental clutter – the half-truths I've held onto, the what-ifs I've rehearsed too many times. Taking the garbage out, in the simplest sense, has become a ritual. A moment where I say to myself, "This doesn't belong here anymore. Let it go." Sometimes that's enough. Sometimes it's the beginning.

In my mind, I often remind myself of what you always say: *"The thing about the past is that it's done. The present is a gift."*

The past used to feel like a leash – one I couldn't find the courage to unclip. But these small rituals, these pauses for release, they help. They remind me that while I don't get to rewrite what's behind me, I do get to decide what I carry onward. And more often than not, the heaviness isn't necessary. It's just old garbage waiting to be taken out.

Not all altered states are born from trauma. Some, I've come to learn, can be chosen. Created. Even welcomed.

The quiet walks, deep breaths, the steady rhythm of the running water over dishes, I find myself slipping into a different kind of awareness. Not numbness, not escape, but a widening of space inside me. It's where old thoughts lose their grip and something softer moves in. A place where healing is allowed and not forced.

These are the spaces where I've learned to listen more closely. Not just to my thoughts, but to what sits beneath them. The fears I've named a thousand times, the grief I didn't think I had the right to feel, the hopes I buried to survive. And strangely, it's in these in-between moments – these trances, that I feel most awake. Most willing to be here. Most able to let go.

Turns out, that's what taking the garbage out really is. Not just clearing the physical clutter or dragging old stories to the curb, but entering that altered space where we realise: *We're not what we've collected. We are what we choose to release.*

So now, every time I take the garbage out, I have you in mind. Of how casually you handed me a metaphor that really stuck and now I cannot live without. You showed me that letting go doesn't always have to be dramatic or painful. Sometimes it's as ordinary as walking something to the curb and deciding not to bring it back in.

I've had to do my own digging, my own clearing. And truthfully, some days I still forget. I catch myself hoarding old thoughts, dragging yesterday into today like it belongs here. But little by little, I remember. I pause. I sort and release. And because of that, I also realise that healing is about noticing when to hold on and when to finally let go.

So, as always, I want to thank you. For being part of that noticing. For helping me begin. And wherever you are today, I hope you're breathing a lot easier too.

With deep appreciation,

FG

Dear FG,

You did it again. Took a casual metaphor and turned it into a compass.

"Taking out the garbage" was never meant to become sacred, but perhaps that's how all rituals begin—with something so ordinary, it becomes invisible. Until someone like you stops, looks, and thinks: *there's something profound in this.*

And there is. Because this practice of yours—the walk to the bin, the mental composting, the rewinding and releasing—is not just about clearing space. It's about protecting what that space is for.

There's an old stone abbey, perched atop a cliff as the storm rolls in. Trees flail. Rain howls. And inside, a flame is being tended. Not because the storm isn't real, but because the flame is. The flame is joy. Love. Wisdom. The right to laugh without shame. To dance without rehearsing your pain. That light inside you—it matters.

And here's the thing. Even the strongest flame flickers in the open. That's why we build lanterns. The lantern is the structure that protects the flame. And the structure isn't grand. It's daily. It's a walk to the kerb. It's the breath you remember to take before reacting. It's the ritual.

Because clarity, despite what Instagram might imply, is not glamorous. It smells a bit like old onions and feels a lot like low-stakes courage. Regular, undramatic, and utterly thankless. That's what makes it sacred. That's what makes it rare.

Joy, contrary to popular belief, does not burst through the door. It sidles in. Sniffs the air. Checks if it's safe. And it only stays if the house is in order—not perfect, just aired out. Not sterile, just clear of emotional takeaway from last Thursday. The prize is not silence. The prize is music. And you have made space for the music to return.

There's something defiant about what you're doing. You're not just maintaining emotional hygiene. You're staging a quiet revolt. In a world that wants you braced, joyless, and cluttered until further notice, you've chosen clarity. You've chosen rebellion. You've chosen love.

You're doing what most leaders forget to do. You're keeping your system clean enough that others don't have to breathe in your stress. And that, my young friend, is the highest form of courtesy I know. You've reminded me of something I once wrote in the margins of a notebook:

The candle is not the point. The light is.

The lantern is not the gift. The warmth is.

The garbage you clear each day—those old rehearsals of shame, of fear, of bracing—is not cleared for its own sake. It's cleared to make room for what we cannot afford to lose.

The light.

The flicker of joy, so easily snuffed. The warm ember of love, glowing beneath grief. The sudden laughter that startles a room back into life. The inner wisdom that returns only when the noise goes quiet. The small pleasure of clean sheets. Of a good plum. Of music through a wall. That's what's being protected.

And it needs protecting, not because it is weak, but because it is precious. Because in a world full of darkness, even a small light shines bright. And in a world filled with light, a few patches of darkness are nothing at all—just contrast, just shade. Nothing to fear. This is why the abbey on the cliff matters. Why we tend the flame.

There will always be storms. There will always be things flung at us —insults, crises, memories that arrive like broken glass. But inside that storm, what steadies us is not the illusion of control. It is the presence of a protected flame. And the knowledge that it is not alone.

Because light is not a solitary thing. One candle doesn't subtract from another. One joy does not threaten another. Light shares. Light spreads. And joy—when protected—becomes contagious. There is a reason the words *heart* and *hearth* are kin. Where there is love, there is warmth. And where there is warmth, there is gathering. That's why we take out the garbage.

So, there is room again for a meal. For a song. For story. For eye contact and clumsy dancing and the kind of laugh that empties the lungs and makes the body forget to brace. The light is not some abstract virtue. It is what reminds us we are alive.

Your letter read like a hymn to that light. And your practice—this daily quiet disposal—is more than personal hygiene. It is a gift you prepare for the future versions of yourself and for the people who will one day lean on you for warmth. Because one day, someone will be cold. Someone will be frightened. And they will find you there—not flickering, not spent, but steady. Because you had the courage to do the small, unimpressive work of keeping the path clear.

Let me be clear: you've out-metaphored me. I've thrown out the odd turn of phrase in my day, but you've walked one to the kerb, thanked it for its service, and left it there like an offering. Now I'll never take out the rubbish again without wondering whether I've also missed the chance to unload a grudge or rinse out a remnant of grief.

But there's something else happening in your letter. Something deeper. You didn't clear space just to feel lighter. You cleared it so something else—something better—could enter. That's the part no one teaches. We speak of decluttering and catharsis as if the goal is emptiness, as if silence is the prize. But you've seen what many miss: we don't clean to be clean. We clean so 'Love' has somewhere to sit down.

You're not emptying your mind. You're preparing a table. For joy. For pleasure. For a moment of peace that doesn't ask you to brace for the next blow. And you've done all this not with flair or drama, but with the quiet determination of someone who no longer needs to prove they're in pain to be taken seriously. Which is why I find myself rereading your words—bin still in hand, door half-closed, breath caught somewhere between inhale and exhale—thinking: this isn't someone coping. This is someone *living*.

You've discovered, without naming it, the secret most people miss. That the emotional rubbish we carry—regret, micro-shame, resentment, fear—doesn't just smell. It ferments. It turns us brittle. It makes our voices sharp and our decisions defensive. And if we don't take it out regularly, we end up storing it in our nervous systems until it finds a leak.

You wrote:

'This doesn't belong here anymore'

And I can't think of a more profound statement of agency. You weren't just clearing space. You were refusing to let rot define the atmosphere of your home, your head, or your heart. This is the kind of leadership no one applauds because they don't see it. But I do. And I'll tell you why it matters.

Because whether you meant to or not, you are becoming the kind of person who offers *regulation-by-osmosis*. One of those rare humans whose breath slows the tempo in the room before they've even opened their mouth. Not because you've 'healed'—god save us from the people who think that word means their 'healing is done'—but because you've created the conditions for others to breathe near you.

You've taken the bin out so others don't have to flinch. That's not self-care. That's service.

Let me say this plainly. Taking out the garbage is not about control. It is about kindling. It is about protecting the flame of what makes us human. We do not do it for tidy minds or personal peace. We do it so the dance can return. So the music can be heard again. So the flame can draw others in. We do it, so joy has somewhere to land. And maybe, just maybe, we do it for this:

"As the clouds leave the sky, we see the moon.

We are no longer scared; we start to run

To group as one; to eat, sing and dance soon.

With our lights conjoined, we become a sun..."

So, keep tending. Keep discarding what no longer serves. Keep making space. Because the world doesn't need more noise. It needs more light. And you, my young friend, have become one of the lantern bearers.

And I hope you know—I'm very proud of you.

With a smile held steady in the storm,

P.

THIRTEEN
AFTER THE FINAL BELL

DEAR P,

I was washing dishes the other day when I suddenly remembered that strange in-between time back when I was still teaching. It was right after the school year ended and we had sent off the students for their vacation. When we returned the following week to finalise grades and submit year-end reports, the school felt unfamiliar. The usual rush of footsteps and echoing voices was gone. The corridors carried some kind of absence. Even the faculty room felt slow.

I remembered sitting at my desk, staring at a checklist I could've easily started, but I didn't move. I wasn't tired or distracted. I just couldn't bring myself to start. I kept thinking that I should felt relieved. But instead, I felt this heaviness that I couldn't explain. As if my mind had been running full speed all year round and suddenly hit a dead end, forgetting how to shift gears or hit the break.

Everything I tried to do felt off. Even the simplest task took longer than expected. And what unsettled me most back then was that nothing was wrong and yet I couldn't feel 'right.'

It was like my brain was so used to sprinting that once the track disappeared, it didn't know how to stop running – or where to run to. It just circled back – running round and round. That moment stayed with me, not because it was painful or anything, but because it was confusing. And because of that I wonder... if feeling stuck is something the brain does, not just something that happens to us, then what does that mean?

I've been thinking more about how the mind gets used to patterns – not just habits, but ways of being. During the school year, my brain had a rhythm. It's used to deadlines, noise, structure, a purpose each day – even when it felt overwhelming. But once that structure vanished, I was left with silence.

But that silence wasn't peaceful. It was disorienting. It was like my brain was searching for the next thing to react to and when it couldn't find one, it defaulted to scanning what was missing. I think in some ways, it was still trying to feel *useful*. So instead of resting, it kept cycling – reevaluating past decisions, inventing new anxieties just to stay active.

Maybe feeling stuck isn't always about being unable to move – it's more like being caught in a fog where nothing feels clear. There's a kind of disconnection that happens, like thoughts are slightly out of reach, or that you're reading lines from a script that used to make sense but now feels hollow. I wonder if this happens when the environment no longer mirrors what the mind expects. When the familiar cues are gone, the brain scrambles to reorient itself. But without context, it questions everything even the most basic decisions. Not because you don't know what to do but because nothing feels meaningful enough to anchor to.

Have you ever seen this happen before? In others, or maybe in yourself? That feeling of being neither here nor there? Not because of circumstances but because the mind seems caught in a fog. Maybe feeling 'stuck' is a pattern the brain runs when it's unsure how to transition.

I'd love to hear how this lands with you. Back then, I was eager to fix the feeling, but now I'm more curious about understanding it. Because I think once we see the pattern, we're no longer inside it quite the same way. And maybe that's where the change can begin.

Warmly,

FG

My Dear FG,

So, the bell rang. The timetable dissolved. The rhythm that had been your heartbeat packed up quietly and left, like a lover with a suitcase and no forwarding address. And there you were—alone in your kitchen, blinking at a kettle you no longer had reason to boil, gripped by a sensation you described—rather poetically—as 'stuck'. You weren't crushed. You weren't broken. You were just... *unrequired.*

Let me reassure you: this isn't burnout. You weren't collapsing. You were hovering. Suspended between roles, like a stage actor in costume with no one calling "places". The kind of post-urgency haze that makes even opening the fridge feel like a decision that ought to involve a team. You didn't fail, FG. You simply forgot to land. And you wouldn't be the first. Allow me to introduce you to an experienced diver called *Gary.*

Gary had twenty years under his belt and the sort of competence that makes laminated checklists seem like an indulgence. He'd once reassembled a valve at 60 metres while quoting Churchill and humming Bach.

But on a Tuesday morning, Gary decided he was too seasoned for lengthy decompression stops. Said he had a lunch booking. Or a dental check-up. Or just an unshakable faith in his own superiority. So, he surfaced. Too fast. As in, *Newton's Law of Regret* too fast.

Ten minutes later, in the carpark, he collapsed—gracelessly, boot half-off, wetsuit tangled like seaweed, bladder making quiet statements of protest. A dive medic murmured something about early-onset Type II. The intern, trying not to smirk, whispered:

'He Gary'd it'

They hauled him inside, damp in the wrong places, pale and vaguely apologetic. When he came to, he blinked and muttered,

'I didn't think it would matter'

Which is precisely what over-functioning people say before becoming cautionary metaphors. The verb stuck. To **Gary**: to resurface too quickly, skip the recalibration, and end up horizontal and humiliated.

Then there's the story of soldier at the supermarket. He'd been back six weeks. Demobbed. Debriefed. Transitioned into suburbia like a good citizen. The camouflage was gone, but the reflexes remained. He entered aisle four of Woolworths to buy chickpeas and left it with a minor concussion and a restraining order from a pensioner.

Here's what happened: a balloon popped. Somewhere near the pasta. And he dropped. Not just a duck, but a full-body tactical engagement. Elbows out. Crackers airborne. Roll manoeuvre into the tinned goods. Aisle Four went silent, apart from the whelping of a small dog. He stood up sheepishly, handed a bent tin to a stunned employee, and said:

'Thought I heard something else'

He didn't return. Not to Woolworths. Possibly not to legumes. But somewhere on the internet, there's a blurry photo captioned: *"Man goes full commando near hummus."*

Because coming home isn't about paperwork. It's about changing state—and knowing when your system is still on patrol.

Finally, there was the diva who lived for ovations. She was radiant onstage. Voice like velvet dipped in voltage. Applause followed her like perfume. Then the curtain fell. The audience vanished. And she found herself backstage in a room with a bar fridge humming like it was trying to self-soothe. Inside: one yoghurt, two hairpins, and her own echo.

She called her agent. Then her therapist. Then a man from her dentist's jazz trio who'd once told her she was luminous. Anything to replace the vacuum. Eventually, she wandered the high street, hoping for recognition or, failing that, a fan with a pulse. She complimented a barista on the café's acoustics. He offered oat milk and aggressive indifference. She wept into a croissant and harmonised with the *Dyson Airblade* in the loo.

She's fine now. Doing Scandinavian voiceovers. Says she enjoys the quiet. But she still claps at toasters. Loudly. You see, when your nervous system learns to survive on ovation, silence feels like exile.

And you, FG?

You've simply exited a high-stakes environment and expected the machinery of meaning to switch off as obediently as your browser tabs. But divers, soldiers, singers, teachers—we all run on cycles. And you can't skip from climax to calm without consequence.

Every seasoned performer knows the arc. The show doesn't start when the curtain rises—it starts with preparation. And it doesn't end with applause—it ends when you've *unbecome* the role you just played. The real professionals know there are five movements:

1. *Arrival* – where curiosity and light readiness get you through the door.
2. *Performance* – sharp focus, flow, muscle memory.
3. *Curtain Call* – soft detachment, the unscrewing of intensity.
4. *Backstage Blur* – slow breath, unstructured hours, the dangerous space where nothing reminds you who you are.
5. *Rehearsal for the Next* – when identity reforms, this time with gentler hands.

You mastered 1 and 2. You skipped 3. And you mistook 4—the quiet phase—for personal failure. But 4 is not failure. It's *dissolution with purpose*. It's where the nervous system exhales. Where the self is restretched, not shrunk. Where we stop performing long enough to find out if anything still lives beneath the script.

The clever professionals don't just finish strong. They *exit skilfully*. They honour the interval. They don't fill the silence with panic. They rehearse the return. They understand this: resilience isn't just holding on. It's *letting go without collapse*.

So here's your prompt, FG. Don't plan the comeback. Plan the re-entry. Not a five-year vision. Just a soft rehearsal. Something to stand on while you change shoes. Let focus return like appetite—not on command. Build structure without urgency. Play music, but don't mistake it for your cue. And when the fog creeps in, don't fight it. Walk with it. Offer tea.

You are not broken. You're just in the airlock between meaningful things. And next time the stillness unnerves you, ask yourself—not sharply, but with the amused affection of someone catching themselves mid-Gary:

Am I broken? Or just between beats?

Then sit. Sip. Watch the kettle steam. And remember: you're not Gary. Not yet, anyway.

Yours in gentle decompression,

P.

FOURTEEN
JUST DREAM ON

DEAR P,

How are you? I hope life is treating you better each day.

Tonight, I've decided to give myself full permission to arrive, not just achieve. Because even on best days, I forget. I forget that I'm not a task to be completed. I'm a person who gets to rest, to feel, to breathe. There's no finish line waiting for me right now, just lovely moments I've been too busy to notice.

Sometimes, I get so zoomed in on what needs doing that I miss the signals my body and mind sent me. A tight jaw, a restless mind, a breath held just a little too long. Those small signs that say, "Slow down. Come back." But I must admit that it takes intention to listen, to really slow down and breathe.

I'm learning that to truly arrive means showing up fully even when that means doing less, being still or simply being gentle with myself. It's not about crossing off another thing on the list as I've thought before. I'm learning the difference between the hustle and the hush.

So, tonight, I'm choosing to meet myself here. Not with expectations or demands, but with kindness and curiosity. To honor what it is, instead of chasing what could be.

I often caught myself in a rush, running from one thing to the next, trying to keep up with everything and everyone. Even when I'm with my friends sometimes, the mere mention of present achievements or future plans would have my mind racing. I forget to simply be present. That's why I'm really set to change that. I want to pause long enough to notice what's right here – in front of me, around me and inside me and let myself have fun with it.

I want to be able to breathe deeply, to feel grounded and just sink to the quiet that often slips away unnoticed. Because when I do that, everything feels clearer and I feel more alive. It's like tuning in to a frequency on a radio that's always there but gets drowned by the noise of daily life. That frequency is where I find myself again, where my thoughts settle, my heart slows, my mind opens just enough to welcome new light.

It's in these moments that I remember what really matters: connection, presence and the simple joy of being here now. And sometimes, that means letting go of control, releasing the need to fix, to plan, to update, to color-code sheets, to do more. To feel the weight of my body on the floor, the rhythm of my breath moving in and out, the warmth of a smile that comes without effort.

I realise that when I lean into this space, however briefly, I carry it forward – into my work, my relationships, my future plans. It becomes something that steadies me. This is the kind of resilience I want to build, not by pushing harder but by coming home to myself.

Just like what you taught me, I'm starting small, just by placing my feet flat on the floor, sitting comfortably and taking full calming breaths. It may sound simple for others, but it's surprisingly powerful. When my feet connect with the ground, I feel a subtle anchor that reminds me: I'm here. Not lost in yesterday's worries or tomorrow's plans, but fully present in this moment.

Because only then do I get to start paying attention to little details I usually overlook. The gentle rise and fall of my chest. The soft sounds in the room. The warm and glorious weather. These are the tiny gifts of presence. These are little reminders that life isn't only about planning and doing, it's also about sensing, feeling and experiencing. When I slow down, enough to see them, I realise how rich even the simplest moments can be.

I remember the first time I held a newborn – so small and fragile, yet somehow already full of life. As I cradled her, time seemed to slow. Her tiny chest rising and falling with each breath, the soft coos and sighs filling the room – all of it felt like a sacred pause in the rush of life. Remembering that, I realised how quickly time moves and how easily precious, fleeting moments slip unnoticed.

It's a vivid reminder that truly living and being present isn't found in the endless lists or plans but in these unrepeatable experiences we often overlook when we're too busy to just be. And that's why I'm learning to slow down. You taught me that this is not escaping the day but creating a state where I can rest, recharge and reconnect. A state that welcomes softness, breathing room and even a little mischief, where my shoulders can drop without needing a permission. This gentle pause becomes a kind of trance built from the colours and light of wisdom and love.

I'm learning to let these lights glow inside me, somewhat like beacons to guide me. I'm learning to trust that this presence, this calm, this kindness toward myself is enough. It's the light that won't flicker out even when there are storms or tough winds. And from this place, I can offer my true self – centered and grounded.

Thank you for sharing your wisdom with me. For helping me see that resilience is about returning home to who I am and will be. I carry this with me now.

And with that, I'll take a deep breath, let my eyes close and settle into the calm knowing that whatever comes next, I'm ready and present.

Trusting the light,

FG

My Young Friend,

You've done more than enough today. So before the world asks another thing of you—let's pause. Let's drop the armour. Let's build a moment made just for you.

You don't have to do anything right now except let your feet be on the floor and take a breath—not a dramatic breath, just one of those sneaky, satisfying ones that shows up when you weren't trying. In through your nose, quick but full, and out through your mouth, as slow as syrup flows.

That's it. That's your signal. We're closing the door on the day now. And if your eyes want to close too—well, they know the routine. They're welcome to follow the rest of you inside. Because this isn't a test. It's a return. It's restoration.

Let your tongue rest heavy on the floor of your mouth, like it's just clocked off a long shift. Let the corners of your mouth think about curving—maybe into a smirk, maybe into the kind of cheeky grin you'd wear when you know something nobody else does. Like the fact that you're about to build a trance-zone, unique to you and all your own.

This one's bespoke. No cold marble or intimidating silence. It's got softness. Breathing room. A faint glow of mischief in the corners. The kind of place that lets your shoulders drop without permission slips. And while we're here, let's bring in some light.

Imagine the top of your head—yes, right there—tingling with the tippy-tip-tip of a finger that knows just how to activate the switch labelled 'clarity'. Whatever colour means clarity to you—sky blue, sunrise gold, or that indescribable hue from your favourite scarf— place it there. Let it glow bright and easy, like a headlamp for the soul.

Then, right at your forehead—centre stage for all your best thinking—let's light up another colour. One that means 'wisdom'. Not the kind printed in manuals or offered unsolicited at dinner parties. The quiet kind. The kind that listens before it answers, that plays the long game. Turn that light on now. Let it stay on.

Feel your tongue again, resting low. Heavy as truth. The back of it soft. Place a colour there, too. This one's for 'deep relaxation'. A hue that tastes like the first sip of something warm on a cold day. Let it spread.

Notice the moisture in your mouth returning. That's your body clocking the shift. Swallow now. And as you do, follow that swallow down to your chest—and switch on a golden light. This one's for love. The sort that doesn't need reciprocation to be real. The kind that's been there since you were small and never left—just went quiet for a while.

Think of someone who's loved you. Not perfectly, but warmly. Let a beam of that golden light reach from your heart to theirs. Watch their face soften. Let it light up. Let it linger. Swallow again. Let the light drop lower. Just one inch below your belly button. That's your joy centre. Not the performative kind. The kind that shows up for no reason—like puddle-jumping in grown-up shoes or singing the wrong lyrics with full conviction. Colour it with joy. Let it fizz like sherbet. Let it spin.

And deeper still. Into the hips. Squeeze and release. Pleasure doesn't need a press release. It just needs permission. There—ignite a flame. Let it move upward: through the belly, through the breath, through the beat of your heart, past your tongue, and straight into your clever mind. Let all those colours, all those lights, align.

Now everything's humming together. Conscious and unconscious, shoulder to hip. You've built something here. A system of self that can glow even in the dark. And as you drift—yes, even further now—

let pieces of dreams and snippets of memory float up. Let your body feel like warm clay, soft and grounded. Let your mind wander to small flashes of wonder: clouds reshaping themselves for your entertainment. The ridiculous joy of bubbles. The first time you saw a rainbow and briefly forgot how to speak.

See yourself smiling. Not for anyone else, but because something in you has come home. See your lights on. Not all blazing at once—just steady. Confident. Warm. Watch people light up around you—not because you performed, but because your presence said, *we're safe here.* And now, see yourself kind. Gently strong. Centred in the middle of your life, not at the mercy of it. Whisper—just in your mind:

That's the person that I am going to be.

That person is *me*!

Then, slowly now... begin to come back. One breath. Then another. Then a third. Let your eyes open when they're ready.

And that's what I wanted to share with you. Not a lesson. Just a lantern and delight.

Now smile. Because for the rests of your life, in many unique styles and in so many beautiful ways, you're going to have many, many a wonderful daze.

SMILE. SPARKLE. SHINE and... just *dream on.*

P.

INTERLUDE—RECLAMATION

There is no ceremony for it.

No soundtrack plays when your body quietly remembers it was never a threat.

No witness claps when the jaw loosens, when the pelvis softens like a door left ajar.

But here it is:

The first desire that doesn't apologise.

The first breath that doesn't brace.

The first flicker of joy

that doesn't ask for clearance.

This is not indulgence. It is repair.

It is your system learning—at last—how to belong to *you*.

Let it.

FIFTEEN
MORE THAN JUST SURVIVING

DEAR P,

"Maybe life should be about more than just surviving, don't we deserve better than that?"

This haunting line from *The 100,* a sci-fi series I've watched a couple years back, has stayed with me since. Spoken in a world ravaged by chaos and politics, it echoed a truth that feels just as relevant now, in our so-called "civilised" lives. Because let's be honest, many of us are surviving. Waking up exhausted, chasing to-do lists, scrolling through filtered-lives, celebrating milestones we never truly chose for ourselves.

We wake up to alarms, pour coffee into multicoloured mugs, and slip into a rhythm that feels more like duty than desire. Days blur into weeks filled with obligations and other responsibilities. And in between, we try to convince ourselves that *we'll get into the good stuff later*. Later, when the timing is right. Later, when there's less chaos. Later, when we've *earned* it. But what if later never comes?

Many of us live like we're invincible – like time is infinite and there will always be another chance, another tomorrow. It's easy to assume there will be time to fix the strained relationship, chase that dream, or finally rest. But the truth is, tomorrow is never promised. It's a sobering thought, buried beneath the noise of our every day lives. And yet, it holds the power to shift everything instantly.

Lately, my feed was peppered with the unexpected. Another road accident. Another person taken too soon by a heart attack, a sudden illness, or a cancer that didn't give any warning. Posts asking for prayers, for strength, for understanding. And just like that, I was reminded of how fragile life really is. It shakes you for a moment... until you scroll on, and the noise of routine swallows the truth again.

Then, there are conversations with my friends – sometimes over lunches, sometimes in the middle of a late-night message that begins with, *"You know what..."* These are the moments that you know would be raw and honest. *"I just want something new," "I need to start over." "I'm so tired of this..."*

They talk about wanting to shift careers, feeling stuck in the roles that no longer feel aligned. Or dreaming of finally starting that project they've shelved for years. Or deciding to go back and finish their master degrees. Some are craving work that feels meaningful, while others just want to breathe without the weight of constant pressure. Many are not even sure what the 'new' is. They miss a version of themselves they can barely remember, one that felt more alive, more curious, more carefree.

But these dreams often stay in limbo – written into journals, saved in notes apps, or spoken in passing only to be quickly brushed aside. There's always a reason to wait: the timing isn't right yet, the bills need paying, the backup plan needs another backup, the uncertainty feels too big. So, they tell themselves "maybe next year" or "once everything is settled." We'd even joke "or maybe even next life..." But next year becomes another year, and things never truly settle.

What's heartbreaking is not that they haven't acted yet – it's that deep down, they're not even sure if they *believe* they can. They've become experts at endurance, at keeping the machine running. Starting over feels risky. So they press pause, not realising how much of life is happening in the background of that waiting.

And yet, when you ask them what they really want, their eyes light up, if only for a second. It's there, under the surface: the longing to feel excited again, to do something that matters, to stop living like they're just getting by. They don't want "more" in the traditional sense. They want real. They want to stop surviving and start living – but don't always know how and where to start.

I know those look and those feelings. Because not so long ago, *them* was me. I was the one saying, "I just need a change", without knowing what that change should look like. I was the one smiling on the outside while asking myself "Is this it?" I kept myself busy, productive and occupied. Deep down I wasn't chasing success, I was searching for something more honest. I want to reignite the passion I once had. But I didn't know how to begin.

I was surviving on autopilot. I envied people who seemed at peace with their lives, people who made decisions with clarity, who laughed without restraint, who focused on things that really mattered to them. I wanted that ease. That purpose. That connection. But instead, like many of us, I kept pushing it aside. I told myself, *later*.

Every now and then, life finds a way to jolt us awake. We pause, shaken, confronted by the reality that life doesn't always offer warnings or extra time. And for a moment, we feel the urgency. The need to live more fully. But then, almost as quickly, we file that urgency under "someday," and return to our routines. It's strange how easily we forget how fragile it all is.

The shift from surviving to truly living doesn't happen all at once. It starts with a decision. It begins in the way you view yourself and the present. It's realising that you don't have to wait until you've arrived somewhere shiny or impressive before you treat your life and the time that you have as something valuable.

I was once tied to a situation that I thought was the end, there was a sense of finality to it.

I often ask:

Is this it? Is this how I'll end up? Am I truly happy or just convincing myself to be?

I was complacent. It looked like security from the outside. It looked like everything I thought I was supposed to want. And for a while, I held onto that tightly and stubbornly despite many people opposing to it, often questioning my decision. Because I believed that letting it go would somehow prove them right. I told myself that no life is perfect, that all commitments come with compromise, that maybe I was just being ungrateful. Later on, I realised that I was only performing a life I thought I wanted.

Looking back now, I don't feel bitterness. Just gratitude for the experience, for what it revealed, and for the courage I somehow found to walk away when everything in me wanted to stay comfortable. I thought it was the end for me. It turns out, it was a beginning I couldn't see yet.

Truly living begins when you start treating the present moment not as a placeholder for something better, but as a place where real life is happening. It's waking up and deciding to show up, enthusiastically but more importantly with intention. Until you slowly notice that the world inside you shifts.

I begin to recognise the voice inside me that says, *"There's more to life than this."* I've finally given myself permission to listen. It should be about feeling things all the way through. Letting myself be moved, even by the smallest things. Enjoy the taste of food, inhale the aroma of freshly brewed coffee in the morning, bob my head along to the beat of the song.

I guess that's the thread running through all this, the reason I started writing this in the first place. Whether it's changing a course, leaving a relationship, or realising that time is moving faster than we think... it all circles back to the same truth: life should be about more than just surviving.

We all have moments of doubts. And sometimes it acts as an invitation for us to take a closer look and ask ourselves, "Is this how I want to live? Have I been settling for less than what I know is possible?" We tell ourselves that we'll come back to the important things later. But *later* is fragile. *Later* is not guaranteed. The only thing we ever really have is *now*. And if we start paying attention to that, we might just find ourselves actually living.

So P, I guess all of this is just my way of saying... I'm beginning to understand the things you used to say. Not just with my mind, but with my life. All your abstract words and metaphors now land differently. I didn't write this to feel validated or anything. I just needed to name where I am now, because I know you'll understand. You always have.

I'm finally beginning to choose differently, think differently and live differently. I don't know where this path leads but I know I want more than survival. I want to live a life that feels real and lived. And I wanted you to know that. Because in your subtle ways, you helped me remember what matters.

Learning to live more fully,

FG

Dear FG,

Some letters arrive like a utility bill. Others like confessions, folded into the corners of silence and sent with the faint hope that someone might care enough to read between the lines. This time, yours arrived like an exhale. The kind that follows years of holding your breath for applause that never came.

You wrote like someone who finally stopped waiting for approval. Not because permission was granted, but because something older and quieter inside you decided it no longer needed it. There's a strange kind of gravity that is revealed by that. Because *Truth* lands heavier when it's been suspended for a while.

I read your letter three times. Not because I didn't get it the first time —I got it immediately—but because the second time, I wanted to feel the shape of the words in my mouth, and the third, because I was bloody well proud of you. Though, don't let that go to your head. Pride is cheap; insight has value.

You didn't just find the language. You found the nerve. And there's nothing more dangerous to *Despair* than a woman who's no longer performing her own silence. Because, let's be honest: most people live like museum exhibits of their former selves—well-lit, tidy, and glassed-off from anything that might ruin the effect. But you walked out of the cabinet. No fanfare. No flash photography. Just the sound of someone returning to their own body.

You see, you were never actually lost. Just slightly misfiled under 'capable' and 'coping'. And now, finally, you've stopped mistaking *functionality* for *fulfilment*. You've quit the holy order of '*Our Lady of Diligent Misery*'. You've thrown out the sermon that said:

'If I keep everyone else comfortable, I might eventually earn joy'.

And now here you are. Fully and inconveniently alive. Which is the best kind of miracle. One that comes with a bit of mischief and a cheeky wee grin.

There's a story that gets handed out like a commemorative mug at induction. You know the one. It's embossed with tasteful ambition, microwavable guilt, and the quiet horror of being praised for your 'reliability'... while your soul screams into a pillow.

The story goes: if you stay busy, they'll leave you alone. If you're productive, they won't ask what you've traded for it. If you delay joy long enough, maybe it'll earn interest. Desire is a liability. Change is indulgent. Starting again? Only if the approval forms come back stamped in triplicate.

That's the great lie. The one everyone tells because the alternative —living honestly—is inconvenient for HR and catastrophic for performance metrics. But underneath the lie, quietly kicking against the lining, is the better joke. The cosmic punchline. The one you only hear when you stop clenching so tightly around your own myth:

You were never meant to manage your way to meaning.

See, the lie sold safety as a lifestyle. And safety, in the commercial sense, is just fear in a better suit. It told you that staying in a misaligned life was noble. That it meant strength. That if you clung to the thing that no longer lit you up, at least you wouldn't be lighting any fires. The joke says otherwise. The joke says:

You get to walk away from the performance mid-scene.

You believed joy must be earned through suffering. That discontent was a lack of gratitude. That feeling good without justification was somehow unethical. But let's be clear—there is no virtue in waiting for the joy police to clear your paperwork.

The people who sold you that story? They're still squinting at spreadsheets and eating sad salad in beige meeting rooms, convinced that if they just get one more promotion, the ache will become applause.

They won't tell you this, because they don't know it yet: Your body already knew the truth. That little twist in your gut? That tightening behind the eyes? That was the part of you still alive, begging not to be buried under another spreadsheet of other people's expectations. And so, while they double-lock their cages and call it security, you've stepped barefoot into the field. Exposed. Uncertain. Gloriously ridiculous. Which, incidentally, is the only place joy can actually find you. The better joke isn't a punchline. It's a pulse. It says:

Feel it now. Want it now. Begin it now.

Because there is no arrival. Just the next moment you decide to feel without flinching.

You used to follow a map. Not one you drew, of course. This was an inherited heirloom—creased, dog-eared, smug. The kind that came laminated in good intentions and riddled with landmarks no one ever actually visited. Security. Achievement. Approval. Settling down, which, as it turns out, often meant '*settling for*'.

And, so, you followed it. Because everyone did. Because someone older said, 'This is the way.' Because saying 'no' sounded a lot like quitting. You drifted into the same cul-de-sacs of compromise, marked your progress with other people's applause, and told yourself the ache was just growing pains. It wasn't. It was misdirection.

Then, quietly, rebelliously, without fanfare—you let it drop. No flaming bonfire of self-actualisation. Just a decision made in the marrow. You stopped pretending the route worked. And there it was: the open space. Not empty. Just undecorated.

You began to write new directions. Not with ink, but in motion. You tasted your morning differently. You walked without rushing. You wanted things again and didn't apologise for it. You didn't need a new map. You just needed to realise you are the compass.

And the old voice—the one that said you needed a five-year plan and a filtered face to feel valid—it still shows up sometimes, doesn't it? But now you answer it with something untranslatable. The softness of your breath. The thrum in your chest. The heat of joy arriving unannounced and uncredentialled. You're writing invitations now. Because now you're not just walking away from the old terrain. You're building a new one. And the rest of us? We're watching the ground grow beneath your feet.

Now comes the hard bit. Not for you—you've already walked barefoot across the gravel of your own self-deception. No, this part's hard because it requires something far trickier than healing: holding the door open for people who don't even know they're locked in. They're not broken. Just over-trained. Experts in restraint. Fluent in delay. Desperate for softness.

You see it in the way they laugh—too loudly, too late. You hear it in the silences between sentences, the way they talk about holidays like war stories, and joy like a risk they can't afford. These are the ones you'll love next. Not by fixing. Just by being. Your joy is not a performance. It's a provocation. Let them watch. Let them wonder. Let them savour the difference in your laughter. Because eventually, some will ask:

'How did you get there?'

And that's when you tell the truth. You used to be one of them. You followed the rules and still felt hollow. You stopped waiting for permission to feel alive. You became a quiet climate shift. And now, others are starting to blush too. You've moved from survivor to orchard keeper. You don't need to drag them into the sun. Just tend your light until they remember where theirs is buried. That's what love looks like at scale. Not grand gestures. Just small warmth, repeated.

The world is changed by people who breathe differently in rooms that forgot how. You already know this. What you've done—this soft, quiet thing of coming back to your own body—isn't lifestyle. It's revolt. Forget chanting affirmations into the abyss. Show me someone who exhales in traffic. Who tastes their dinner. That's the revolution.

It begins in the kitchen. On the commute. In the pause before you answer a question you used to rush through. You've done this already. I saw it in the letter you didn't edit. I felt it in the gaps between your paragraphs. That's the sound a body makes when it stops performing survival. There's no badge. No parade. Just a growing clarity. Your calm is not surrender. It's knowing exactly where you stand—without needing to raise your voice.

Some will hate it. Some will try to fix it. But some—jeez, some—will lean toward you like moths to a door left ajar. Not because you offered them light, but because you reminded them they have a switch.

So, here's your final assignment:

Don't abandon your nervous system for anyone. Not the ones who say you're too much. Not even the 'older you' who thought peace was a prize for good behaviour. You're allowed to feel good now. Not because you earned it. Because you exist. Because it's your birthright.

You are the author now. And authors don't need permission. They need paper. And a bit of quiet. And sometimes, a reader who reminds them that the blank page isn't a threat—it's a door. Walk through that door. Leave it ajar. Let it be silent invitation for others to find home.

Live in such a way that your body doesn't have to whisper to get your attention anymore. You've listened. You've changed the weather. You'll be the reason someone remembers how to feel again. That's more than surviving. It's the whole damn miracle. No trumpet. No crowd. Just a kettle clicking off. And the low hum of ordinary life, resuming.

Somewhere along the line, you stopped auditioning. You let go of the story where permission must be earned and pain is the entry fee for peace. You started living in your body like it was home. Which is exactly how real power works.

And you? You've become one of those rare people who can sit in a room full of chaos and not try to fix it. Just be in it, like the furniture, quietly radiating coherence. That's impact. Not applause. Atmosphere.

Of course, you'll forget again. That's the game. But then you'll feel it. And you'll remember. Not in a thunderclap. In the laugh you let out that's so unguarded it startles even you. That's the return. Not to who you were. But to who you were underneath the noise. No more waiting. You've come back to your life. You'll always find home. And you'll do it again. Every time you forget. And if someone asks what you're doing these days, you can tell them the truth.

"I'm living".

P

P.S. You never needed a lighthouse—just a wee nudge to dazzle without permission. Now nudge someone else who's still too well-mannered to glow.

A NUDGE TO THE ONE STILL HOLDING THIS BOOK

Only to name what had gone too long unspoken. Only to reach across the silence and find one steady hand. But this book is not the end.

It's the breath before your letter begins. Because somewhere—in a staffroom, a bedroom, a classroom long after the bell—someone else is aching for the words you haven't written yet.

So if the thought emerges, tender and half-formed—

Could I say something too?

Yes. Write it. Whether in ink, in voice, in gesture, in rest, in the life you now choose to live more completely—that letter will count.

And if no one else says it today, let us say it here:

"We've been waiting to hear what only you can say."

AFTERWORD

P—

Let's not pretend anything's been 'resolved'. If you've gotten this far, you're not looking for resolution anyway. You're looking for something more useful:

> *A kind of companionship that doesn't flinch when*
> *things wobble.*

What these letters offer—if they offer anything—isn't a roadmap. It's a rhythm. A pacing beside you. Someone who doesn't rush ahead with bullet points or lag behind with hindsight.

Teaching—like living—isn't a craft you finish. It's something you perform while the roof leaks, the bell rings, and the best part of your lunch is stolen by Year 9.

And leadership—the kind rooted in care, not control—is rarely rewarded and frequently misread. So, if you're feeling slightly frayed, quietly heroic, and not entirely sure what's next... good. You're exactly where you need to be.

We've spoken about stillness. About stress. About that maddening zone between *fine* and *falling apart*. What we haven't said—at least not outright—is this:

The work you do matters.

Not in a poster-quote way. In a visceral, biological, someone's-nervous-system-is-watching-you kind of way.

<u>You</u> are the context in which others learn to breathe.

So, no, you don't need more strategies. You need more mercy. Start there.

There's an old superstition among the seasoned ones—those who've seen enough to lose the shine but not the spark—that when you make it to the end of a thing, you should look back and nod.

- Not to say *I nailed it.*
- But to say *I stayed.*

You did. And that counts. Now put the book down. Go breathe. And if you must carry anything forward, let it be this:

The best leaders glow slightly. Not because they're radiant—but because they've spent time in the dark, and they remember the way out.

FG—

Thank you for walking this far with me.

These letters have been a mirror I didn't know I needed – sometimes soft and flattering, sometimes painfully honest and clear. But always kind. They helped me see the truths I'd been overlooking, and reminded me that honesty, even when it's uncomfortable, is another form of care.

If something here helped you soften, steady or see yourself more clearly, I hope you'll write back. Not necessarily to me, but maybe to yourself. Or to someone who needs your truth, your presence, your permission to be real.

Because more than anything, I hope this reminds you:

You don't have to just survive.

You don't have to pretend you're okay to be loved or worthy or seen.

Life is waiting, but I'm afraid not so patiently. It wants your full presence. It wants you here and now. And not as a version of who you think you should be, but as you are.

Let this be your permission to begin again. To choose living. To choose becoming.

Letter change people. Especially the ones we're finally brave enough to live.

June 2025

ACKNOWLEDGMENTS

My thanks to the teachers and mentors whose wisdom has shaped me —and, through me, those I now have the privilege to guide.

To **shī Wú Qiàqí**: for teaching me that *"problems don't care about your skillset. They're going to keep happening until you have a skillset that can solve them."* And for helping me understand another people, another language, another time. These pages drip with your quiet charm and fierce clarity.

To **Tim Dalmau**: for your cognitive heft and generous guidance. As friend and mentor, you offered both depth and distance—always when I most needed it. Your ability to see both the forest and the leaf, simultaneously and without strain, left an indelible imprint.

To **Stephen Porges**: whose Polyvagal insights whisper beneath every line. The arc of this book—breath by breath—is your beautiful science of safety, made human.

And finally, and most heartfelt, to the one and only **Richard Bandler**: whose hypnotic use of poetic meter, rhyme, and humour delivered more than techniques—it delivered permission to be more than I had become. You radiate embodied wisdom, cloaked in laughter. For that, and for it all, I shall remain ever in your debt.

—P.

ABOUT THE AUTHORS

 **Paul O'Neill** is trusted by professionals in business, heavy industry, medical and mental health, and elite sports as a consultant, coach, and guide. For more than twenty-five years, he's been doing exactly that: guiding individuals, teams, and entire organisations through the thickets of change, chaos, and contradiction with a calm intensity that refuses to settle for surface solutions.

His leadership and coaching record spans continents and industries, yet his work never follows a formula. That's the point. Real transformation, he insists, can't be imposed or standardised. It must be built, brick by deliberate brick, in the language, rhythm, and logic of those who live it.

Clients across Australia, New Zealand, the UK, North America, and South Africa describe him as 'visionary', 'invaluable', 'a lifelong friend'—though the word most often repeated is 'transformational'. Not because Paul performs miracles, but because he hands the tools over. He trains people to recognise patterns, to respond to pressure with composure, to build resilience that sticks—not just in the individual nervous system, but in the culture of entire teams.

Francinne Kaye Gacilo brings the heart of a teacher to everything she does – whether in the classroom or behind the scenes of digital transformation. A licensed educator by training, she later transitioned into the dynamic world of digital media and content development. Before stepping into the world of teaching, she gained firsthand experience in the corporate environment where she learned the true value of collaboration, adaptability and showing up even when the script runs out.

That transition shaped more than her resume. It shaped her worldview. Working with teams, leading projects and mentoring others revealed not just the challenges young professionals face, but the inner battles of self-doubt, burnout, and the need to belong.

Francinne writes and works from lived experience, blending curiosity with compassion, structure with soul. Her contribution to this work is a reflection of her deep belief: that resilience is not a trait we're born with, it is something that we build slowly and practice daily through ordinary moments, difficult choices and persistence to keep showing up.

ALSO BY PAUL O'NEILL

Back into Delight

The Iron Laws

Grounded, Bonded & Flowing

Neuro-Resilience Skills series

Vol. 1: The Inner Game of Leadership

Vol 2: The Outer Game of Leadership

NLP Mastery for Leaders series

Vol 1: Adaptive Wisdoms

Vol 2: Logic & Language

Vol 3: Moving As One

Six Pillars of Successful Executives

Pillar 1: Personal Resilience

Pillar 2: Non-Verbal Cues

Pillar 3: Pristine Problem Solving

Pillar 4: Impactful Speaking

Pillar 5: Engagement Excellence

Pillar 6: Strategic Resilience

Printed in Dunstable, United Kingdom

71330110R00095